Life's Ultimate Privilege

DeVern Fromke

Life's Ultimate Privilege

DeVern Fromke

SF ISBN 0 9365 95-01-9

87 88 89 90 91--8-7-6-5-4-3

How This Started

For years I wanted to.

I knew the importance.

I struggled again and again to be diligent. But I never maintained a devotional life consistently.

I really longed for more intimate fellowship with God, but I was a failure. I knew it! And I was ashamed! I justified my failure in many curious ways.

Then I reached a crisis!

One day I realized I had been in active ministry 40 years. Strangely, the one thing I emphasized so often—intimate fellowship with God —was still so lacking in my life. My shame, my failure, my hyprocrisy grew like a shadow before me! Even the constant demand as a teacher speaking before large audiences across the country gave me little comfort.

I was failing God . . . and man!

Then warning came! It was as though the Lord spoke to me: "My son, if you don't start now . . . you never will." I knew that was so true! I was, it seemed, about to make an irrevocable choice: either I could lag along, and my failure would become more apparent, or I could choose fullness of fellowship.

A desperation cry came from deep within: "Father, I will! I must meet You livingly every day, but I ask that you take me home if I do not fulfill this calling to a hidden life with you—before all other ministry."

I turned a corner that day. I knew (intuitively) things would be different! These past three years have been very different! Some of the lessons I am learning will be shared in this journey we are taking together.

Thanks for your understanding . . . and your desire to join me.

Preparing For Our Journey!

I HOPE YOU LIKE STORIES!

IT WILL BECOME EVIDENT that for each day of our journey we have chosen a true-life situation, so as to capture your attention, to appeal to your emotions, to enlighten your mind, but primarily to strengthen your will. We make no apology for using these heart-warming stories to illustrate some vital principles.

NORMALLY, WE ENCOURAGE everyone to start his devotional time by reading God's Word as a preparation for prayer-fellowship. Yet this ideal method does not always stimulate beginners to get started. Since this journal is primarily designed for beginners, we are attempting to first capture interest and then lead into God's Word. For those who have already established a fruitful time of fellowship with the Lord, this will seem very elementary.

THIS IS NOT an ordinary book intended to be read through in a couple sittings. Rather, it is written as a journal for our 15 day journey together. I thank you for not reading ahead and rushing through it in a few hours. You will discover that the greater value is not so much in the contents, as in the daily discipline you will develop. May I repeat—the discipline you develop to daily fellowship with God is most important.

IT IS COMMON KNOWLEDGE that in doing something 21 times, a habit is formed. If no other good comes from this journal, we want to help you start the habit of consistently meeting God in fellowship each day. In these 15 days you will be well along in establishing the best habit we know. Imagine—fifteen times—the Lord will have had first place in your life. We are sure you will continue the rest of your life.

LEARN TO ORGANIZE the rest of your day around your appointed time of fellowship. Don't let the activities of the day decide this time. Fix a time and let it stay fixed, so that each day you do not have to debate the question of when, or where, or how to proceed. If at all possible, fix the time early in the morning. If you fix the time at night you will be *backward-looking*. If you fix the time in the morning you will be *forward-looking*, as the Psalmist says:

"My prayer comes to thee in the morning" (Ps.88:13).
"I sing of thy strength, a morning song to thy love" (Ps.59:16).
"Morning by morning He awakens me to learn my lesson " (Isa.50:4).
"I am up before the dawn to pray, waiting for thy promises" (Ps.119:147).

You are fresher in the morning and can more easily receive. But whatever time you select, do fix it for regularity.

REMIND YOURSELF that God is more concerned than you for developing this daily fellowship. As you begin each day, pray for help. You are beginning a discipline which will make the difference between weakness and strength, between defeat and victory. He will surely answer your cry:
Lord ... AWAKEN MY HEART ... TODAY!

Why is Fellowship Such a Privilege?

Can you imagine the excitement of being invited for a private appointment with the President of the United States. Very few of us will ever have that honor or privilege. Yet the God of the universe invites all His children for a private appointment and allows them to enter His presence for unrestricted fellowship. WHAT A PRIVILEGE!

But even more! This God encourages us to spend much time with Him, allowing us to **know Him** intimately and enjoy unhindered communion with Him. WHAT A PRIVILEGE!

But even more! This God has arranged His plans, so as to invite us to **participate with Him** in accomplishing His eternal purpose. When we think of this we are almost breathless. WHAT A PRIVILEGE!

But even more! God calls us to be so identified with His WAYS that we can become **partners with Him** in living unto fullness. This is indeed the ULTIMATE PRIVILEGE. For us to really appreciate the theme of this journal, it will be helpful if we understand that...

LIFE'S ULTIMATE PRIVILEGE is wrapped
up in this word: FELLOWSHIP (koinonia).

This Greek word, koinonia, is a very inclusive word, which in translation requires several English words to give the full meaning. Let us consider these four aspects of fellowship:

WE CAN MEET WITH HIM DAILY:
"...and truly our **fellowship** is with the Father, and with His Son Jesus Christ" (1Jn.1:3). also Prov.8:34, 1Cor.1:9

WE CAN COMMUNE WITH HIM INTIMATELY:
"If you have any encouragement from being united with Christ, if any comfort from his love, if any **fellowship** with the Spirit, if any tenderness and compassion... (Phil.2:1 NIV). also Gen.18:17

WE CAN PARTICIPATE IN HIS PURPOSE:
"...to make all men see what is the **fellowship** of the mystery... according to the eternal purpose which he purposed in Christ Jesus our Lord..." (Eph.3:9,11). also Rom.8:28; 2Tim.1:9; Heb.2:6,7

WE CAN BECOME PARTNERS WITH HIM:
"I want to know Christ and the power of his resurrection and the **fellowship** of sharing in his sufferings..." (Phil.3:10 NIV). also 1Cor.3:9

Now, let us begin our journey together!

CONTENTS

Introduction

DAY ONE

DURING THESE BEGINNING DAYS your fellowship with God may seem more like a duty than a privilege. Don't be alarmed! That will change! As you come to know and love Him more, your desire to fellowship with Him will greatly increase. You will come to realize He is worthy of the time you have committed to Him each day.

So, while making a commitment to God comes first, the discipline for keeping that commitment will need to be developed. This will give God opportunity to develop character in you. Since He is concerned for this, we can count on His help.

IN THIS FIRST LESSON, we consider two questions:

Why is a "full rescue" so imperative?

Why is running life's race equally important?

We must recognize that many who attempt to run the "race of life" have never been fully rescued. Others who have been rescued fail to understand the distinctive purpose God has for each of us in running life's race. Only as we are clear in this, can the following lessons in our journey be meaningful.

So, let us begin with prayer and the confidence that God will bring us into a fuller understanding of life's ultimate privilege:

Father, we thank Thee for eyesalve so as to see more clearly; for a teachable spirit to receive insights we have not considered before; and for a supply of grace enabling us to be more diligent than ever before. In the name of the Lord Jesus we pray. Amen!

OUR STORY, reportedly a true incident, is from the SUNSHINE MAGAZINE. We appreciate the opportunity to publish this somewhat abridged account.

The Rescue and the Race

LEIF OLAFSON ate his early-morning breakfast in silence, and Mary, his wife, served him quietly, for both were thinking of the day that lay ahead.

Leif had not been fishing for several weeks due to the heavy storms that had lashed the Alaskan coast near Petersburg. His small but sturdy fishing boat was no match for the giant seas that rolled in along the rocky shore. Now the storms had finally abated, and weather forecasts were for good fishing weather. It was very important that he get some good catches, for fishing constituted his means of livelihood.

"Well, so long, Honey!" exclaimed Leif as he pushed back his chair, shouldered his provision box, gave Mary a warm hug and kiss, and strode out into the night.

Arriving at the dock, Leif quickly loaded his gear, started the motor, and skimmed over the water toward the fishing grounds. He carefully avoided several icebergs, which had recently broken loose from the glaciers that extended out into the sea, remembering that seven times as much ice lay invisible beneath the water as that which he could see. Leif had seen bigger boats than his crushed by the hidden portion of a huge berg.

But this morning, as the sun came over the edge of the world, he was carefree, and the echoes rang to his songs as he worked his way through the passages between the many rugged islands of the southeastern Alaskan coast. He had caught several sizeable fish by early afternoon, and was feeling tired but happy when suddenly— swish! Something had his hook, and it was off and running. . . .

It must be a big fellow, for sure! He laid out all the line and handled the boat as skillfully as he could. His whole body tingled with the joy of the chase. One hour, two hours went by. He had caught several glimpses of his prey. A grand king salmon!—must weigh fifty pounds or more.

Finally, the fish was worn out, and Leif drew him alongside, gave him the fatal blow, and dragged the salmon into the boat. What a beauty! Leif straightened up to look around. He gasped!

In the struggle with the fish, the boat had drifted dangerously close to a huge iceberg. He jumped to start the motor, but even as he moved, he heard a rumbling noise and suddenly felt himself being lifted—boat and all—out of the water! Suddenly he was high in the air. His boat was evidently resting on a projecting shelf of the iceberg. The great iceberg had tilted and raised the ledge with his craft upon it!

As suddenly as it had started, the motion stopped. The boat, still right side up and level, rested some thirty feet above the water! The angle was so precarious that any movement on Leif's part could easily cause some further tilting. He hardly dared to breathe.

The sun had sunk low in the sky when suddenly he heard the sound of a motor above him—the evening mail plane. As it flew overhead, he waved carefully. The wing dipped, and the plane circled once, then again. There was no way the pilot could land, no way to help him except to send a boat . . . but could they reach him in time?

Leif settled down for the night. No one could help him now. Perhaps no one ever could! Mary would hear what had happened, and would know that his chances were slim. She would pray. Mary did such things. She seemed to get results too. In his present predicament, this really did seem pretty reasonable. His mother too, had believed in such things and had sent him to Sunday school regularly.

Before he fully realized it, Leif found himself speaking aloud. "Lord God, could You help me tonight? If You could give me the chance to get back to Mary and little John, I'd never forget it, God. I promise to take You into my heart and trust You, as Mary does. This is a job I can't handle alone, God."

A strange calm came over Leif, and he relaxed there in the boat. In the still night, the stars shone clear and beautiful.

He must have dozed, for suddenly he roused to the sound of a motor. He could see a small boat approaching. Gratefully, he recognized the Coast Guard cutter.

All at once, he thought he felt a tremor. There was a slight movement—he was tipping toward the water! The movement increased rapidly—toward the water. Before he could believe his senses, the little boat shot out over the water, kept its balance, as it flew away from the berg.

At that very moment Leif heard a shout from the approaching Coast Guard. "Well, if I hadn't seen that myself, I never could have been made to believe it happened!" shouted the captain. "What kind of charm do you wear?"

Leif started to answer lightly, but his voice caught. He spoke slowly. "There was no charm. It was a miracle—an answer to prayer. God can control an iceberg just like He controlled those waves of long ago."

The captain saw a strange glow on Leif's face. His own heart gave a queer leap. "Guess you're right, fellow. Don't believe you can ever forget such an experience."

"No," responded a new and humbled Leif. "My life will never be the same."

We are told that Leif returned to his home with a new serenity and an inward peace. From that day onward, men who knew Leif Olafson said he was a different man. No matter what situation or emergency arose, he was always calm and confident. He seemed to live by an Inner Resource.[1]

What an amazing rescue! For Leif it meant not only a rescue from immediate death, but even more—a "spiritual" rescue from eternal death. Perhaps we should consider that a bit more.

There are many today, like Leif, who are not aware of any need of spiritual rescue, that is until such an emergency arises. For them, life has, indeed, had its ups and downs, but they go on quite unconcerned about their deepest need, until . . . until they are faced with death and eternity. Then the all-important question faces them:

Are they ready to meet their God?

In that moment of facing death, everything looks so different! This is God's moment to break in—His opportunity. Wealth and fame, health and ambition—all these things previously so important, become insignificant in the scale of eternal values.

No one can know all that passed through the mind of Leif during that long night. We do know that he had much more time to consider than do most folk. Possibly he remembered how he had ignored God and selfishly lived for his own purposes. Sure, he was "good and honest", respected and moral—at least most people considered him to be so. Yet inwardly Leif knew that he had been running from God all these years. Now God had caught up with him.

Perhaps living with a wife like Mary had convinced him that God could change a life. He remembered how Mary had changed since she trusted Christ as her Savior. Was it too late for him? He was at least hopeful that God would hear her many prayers for him—if not his own pleading.

So Leif made that great surrender! For him this was to be no mere trial, but a life-long promise to God. He knew that now he belonged to God, and God belonged to him. He felt forgiven and cleansed of all his past, and stood on the only promise he could recall from his boyhood days. "... Whosoever shall call on the name of the Lord shall be saved" (Rom.10:13). It was just that simple; he had called. God had heard ... and saved him. He knew he was a changed man with a new outlook on life.

THE GREAT TRAGEDY THAT OFTEN FOLLOWS

All of us who have been rescued have actually just reached the starting point of our race. Our rescue is wonderful, for we have been forgiven, set free from our past and have been placed in God's family. But being a Christian involves more than a "rescue operation". There is a race to be run, a life-purpose to be fulfilled. For our new life to have meaning, value and direction, we must do more than ...

> *look back* (at our rescue), we must
> *look forward* to life's purpose.

Paul wrote to young Timothy:

> You are not only rescued because of
> His grace, but you were rescued in
> order that you might fulfill His purpose
> (2 Tim. 1:8-9).

Yes, it is a tragedy that multiplied thousands who have been rescued hardly recognize that they are called unto purpose; hence they make little progress.

We need to understand why!

We need to recognize God's warning.

Our real concern as we begin this journey together is to ask God to so AWAKEN OUR HEARTS that we might clearly understand what it means to run life's race—not somehow—but triumphantly.

To understand this we must see an over-view of God's dealing with man since that first day when God created Adam and placed him in the Garden of Eden. We have pictured Adam standing at a

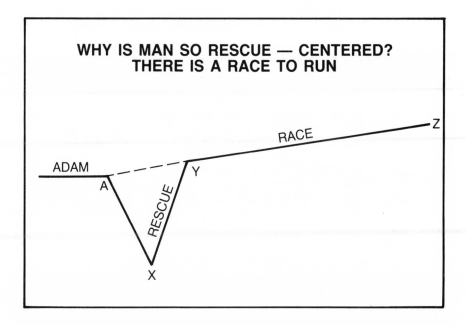

WHY IS MAN SO RESCUE — CENTERED?
THERE IS A RACE TO RUN

gateway of choice: either to go God's way (a to z) or to go his own way (a to x). From the beginning it was in God's plan for Adam (and all mankind) to yield to Him for fulfilling His purpose; thus Adam would be sustained by the divine Life-union with God. It seems evident that the source for that Life-union was available to man in the garden, as represented by the Tree of Life. This would be the only Life-source by which Adam could run the race and fulfill God's purpose. While Adam had never yet eaten of that Tree of Life, no doubt he could have eaten, once the issue of committing himself to God for His purposes, had been settled.

> *Here was the critical issue: Adam was either to live*
> *(dependently) by the Tree of Life, or to live*
> *(independently) by eating of the tree of knowledge.*

And we must face it; the same issue remains for each of us today. Either we:

LIVE BY HIS LIFE, or we

LIVE BY OUR OWN (SOUL) LIFE.

We must understand that what Adam did, in his own rebellion, we have also done. Actually we, like Adam, have all chosen to go our own way. "All we like sheep have each turned to his own way ..." (Isa.53:6). This means we are not only sinners by our own choice, but (in Adam) we are also sinners by nature. Because of our relationship with Adam as our representative head, we will reap the sure harvest from sin . . . death. However, once we have a new relationship with Christ, we have the sure promise of His Life.

As we have pictured, God provided the way of rescuing Adam from his fallen condition (x to y). Through the redemptive work of His Son on the Cross, He redeems us by blood, which obtains forgiveness for our sins and disobedience. But He also provides access to His Son (the Tree of Life). As He quickens our human spirit, we receive His divine Life (Tree of Life). . . we are born anew. (Eph.2:1; Jn 1:13)

What a rescue!

Surely it will take all eternity to understand and appreciate the completeness of our rescue. The apostle Peter explains how God has provided two incorruptible things:

BLOOD which gives us redemption, and the
SEED OF GOD'S WORD which gives us eternal life.
(1 Pet. 1:18-23)

It is little wonder that down through the centuries mankind continues to appreciate this rescue-operation. As with countless others, no doubt Leif never tired of telling about his own rescue from the iceberg, but even more important—his rescue from sin and eternal death. Who would ever minimize the importance of God's rescue-operation?

Yet there is something most tragic!

All too often man becomes so "rescue-centered" that running "life's race" becomes almost obscured. The glory of redemption would seem to outshine the glory of God's original purpose in creating man. Surely God did not place man here just to rescue him! Man did not need to sin so that God would have someone to save (rescue)! We must be careful here! While our full redemption is imperative, it is equally imperative and glorious that we run the race triumphantly for His glory.

God originally purposed for man to RUN THE RACE, that is, live with a total dedication to fulfill God's ultimate intention for Himself. The tragedy of man's awful sin and failure in no way changes God's original purpose. When the need arose, God merely incorporated this need for man's rescue into His over-all plan.

The all-important question now is, when are we going to move beyond a pre-occupation with our own rescue and become occupied with running the race, so as to fulfill God's eternal purpose?

As we progress in this 15 day journey we shall see how important it is that each of us has appropriated all God intended in His rescue-operation: Life, peace, cleansing, victory, deliverance, etc. But we are equally concerned that God will receive His inheritance (Eph. 1:14,18) as His children live unto fullness of purpose

WHAT MAN NEEDS ... is important!
WHAT GOD RECEIVES ... is most important!

QUICKENING FROM YOUR WORD.... Heb. 12:1-15

In closing each lesson we shall consider some portion of God's Word for continuing meditation throughout the day. From the above reading we select this phrase:

> *".. . let us run with patience*
> *the race that is set before us" (vs 1).*

Have you ever "chewed" on a verse or phrase during the hours of a day, and God gave you new insights and strength you had not expected? Try it now! What does "run" mean? What does "race" mean? What does "patience" mean? Since Jesus has already run His race and won, how can He help us? How much patience can I expect Him to supply for today's trials? What does the writer mean by "set before us"? Once you have learned to "carry" a verse in your heart, and ponder it all day, you will never again be without some "grist for your mill".

AWAKEN MY HEART.... to really understand Life's race.

Father, each day I shall ask You to stretch my heart so I can experience an increasing measure of fellowship with You. Already today I am beginning to see how much my life has been centered in what I have wanted to get from You, rather than in what You might receive from my life, as I live wholly for Your pleasure and purpose.

Forgive me, Father! I did not realize how much I had been occupied with my own needs, my problems, my projects. I know You expect me to claim Your full rescue in every area of my life. I do reckon upon all that the Lord Jesus accomplished on the cross for my rescue. I do thank You for forgiveness, and for placing Your Life in me. Whenever You unveil some deeper aspect of the rescue which needs yet to be operative in me, I shall thank You.

BUT FATHER, I WANT MUCH MORE!

I want nothing to hinder my running the race and winning the prize, as Paul exhorts us in 1 Cor. 9:24-26 and Phil.3:14.

OVERFLOWING GRATITUDE!

Each day we shall close our lesson by singing together some familiar hymn, or message of praise which expresses our joy, our thanks, our adoration, our appreciation for fellowship with Him. At this point it seems my heart wants to burst forth in rejoicing.

Will you join me in singing that familiar melody: (Come Thou Fount of every Blessing). I am adding my own words in these first eight lines.

Since my rescue from destruction
    Like a bird, I am set free;
Free to offer full devotion,
    To the One Who now owns me.

Lord, I see the race before me,
    One which You've already run;
Now You beckon me to follow,
    Other saints who've gone above.

Come, Thou fount of every blessing,
    TUNE MY HEART to sing Thy grace,
Streams of mercy, never ceasing,
    Call for songs of loudest praise.

Teach me some melodious sonnet,
    Sung by flaming tongues above;
Praise the mount—I'm fixed upon it
    Mount of Thy redeeming love.

Oh to grace how great a debtor,
    Daily I'm constrained to be!
Let Thy goodness, as a fetter,
    Bind my wand'ring heart to Thee;

Prone to wander, Lord, I feel it—
    Prone to leave the God I love—
Here's my heart, oh, take and seal it—
    Seal it for Thy courts above.
              (R. Robinson)

_____
_____
_____
_____
_____
_____
_____
_____
_____
_____
_____
_____
_____
_____
_____
_____
_____
_____
_____
_____
_____
_____
_____
_____
_____

Questions for further study

In the past, which has been most important for me? My personal rescue or running the race? Why? _____

_____

Could it be that many of God's children are hobbled in running the race, because they have never appropriated the "fullness of their rescue?" What are the essentials in our rescue?_____

_____

Two New Testament Scriptures speak of the race. (Heb. 12:7, 1 Cor.9). My rescue is by grace—the gift of God, but running the race will qualify me for the prize? What is the prize?_____

_____

DAY TWO

IN THE PAST YOU MAY HAVE WONDERED why you were making so little progress in your prayer-life? You have prayed and prayed, yet God hasn't seemed to answer? You have pondered whether your faith was too weak, whether your deepest motives were right, or if you were really asking according to God's will? At this point you have even begun to lack confidence in prayer, and though you have been keeping a daily appointment with God, you know there has actually been very little fellowship with Him.

You are not alone! Multitudes are asking this same question. But there is help today. First, we must uncover some of the reasons for our failure.

IN TODAY'S LESSON we ask this question:

How is it possible for someone to go through the daily routine of Bible reading and prayer, yet actually fall short of that fellowship which God most desires?

We shall see that our appointment times with God must be more than bringing our daily "want list." If we are to make any real progress in life's race we must become PURPOSE-CONSCIOUS. This means our praying must focus on what God is ultimately after; then we shall begin to realize why God is ever pressing us to a partnership with Himself. Yes, we shall begin to understand that there is something better than getting answers to our prayers.

OUR STORY related by Dr. D.M. Stearns will surely encourage you in praying for unsaved members of your family and give you renewed confidence in God's faithfulness.

Something More
Than Answers

MANY YEARS AGO at a Bible conference, the late Dr. D.M. Stearns had a question hour. One of the questions handed to him read:

"If you had prayed all your life for the salvation of a loved one, and then you got word that that person had died without giving any evidence of repentance—having lived a sinful life—what would you think, both of prayer itself and of the love of God and His promise to answer?"

It was a striking question, and everyone in the room wondered how he would respond.

"Well, dear sister," he began, "I should expect to meet that loved one in heaven, for I believe in a God who answers prayer, and if He put that exercise upon your heart to pray for that dear one, it was because He, doubtless, intended to answer it."

Then he told this story:

Many years ago there was a dear mother in Philadelphia who had a very wayward son. This young man, though brought up in the church, had never trusted Christ and had drifted into everything unholy. He had gone to sea and had become a very rough, careless, godless sailor.

One night his mother was awakened with a deep sense of need upon her heart. When fully awake, she thought of her son and was impressed that he was in great danger; as a result, she got up and prayed earnestly that God would undertake for her boy, whatever his need was.

She didn't understand it, but after praying for several hours, there came a sense of rest and peace, and she felt sure in her heart that God had answered. Getting back into bed she slept soundly until the morning. Day after day she kept wondering why she had been awakened and had been moved to prayer, yet somehow she could not feel the need to pray for her son any more; rather she praised God for something which she felt sure He had done for him.

Several weeks passed. One day the mother heard a knock at the door. When she opened the door—there stood her son! Entering the room he announced, "Mother, I'm saved!" Then he told her this amazing story.

He explained how a few weeks earlier, his ship had been tossed in mid-Atlantic by a terrific storm, and there seemed no hope of riding it through. One of the masts had snapped, and the captain called for the men to move out to cut it away. As they stepped out, he among them, cursing and reviling God because they had to be out in such an awful night cutting away this mast, suddenly the ship gave a lurch. A great wave caught the young man at that moment and swept him overboard.

As he struggled helplessly with the enormous power of the sea, the awful thought came to him, "I'm lost forever!" Suddenly he remembered a hymn that he had often sung in his boyhood days:

> There's life in a look at the crucified One.
> There is life at this moment for thee:
> Then look, sinner, look unto Him and be saved;
> Unto Him who was nailed to the tree.

He cried out in agony of heart, "Oh God, I do look. I look to Jesus." In that moment he was carried to the top of the waves and lost all consciousness.

Hours afterwards when the storm had subsided, and the men came out to clear the deck, they found him lying unconscious, crowded against a bulwark. Evidently, while one wave had carried him off the deck, another had carried him back again. The sailors took him into the cabin and gave him restoratives. When he came to, the first words from his lips were, "Thank God, I'm saved!" From that hour on he had an assurance of salvation that meant everything to him.

Having finished his story, the mother then told her son how she had prayed for him that very night. They discovered it was exactly at the time when he was in such a desperate plight that God had heard and answered.

"Now suppose," Dr. Stearns continued, "that young man's body had never been brought back to the ship. Suppose he had sunk down into the depths. People might have thought he was lost forever in his sin, but God in His loving kindness not only saved him, but permitted him to come back and give testimony of God's wonderful saving grace."

While we recognize this answer to prayer was sovereignly made known, we must also realize that there are other answers to prayer we shall never know about until we meet our Lord.[1]

In her years of patient praying for a wayward son, this mother was discovering that God is wholly trustworthy in answering her prayers, but He is . . . .

SOMEONE MORE THAN AN ANSWERER.

He is more concerned that we come to know and trust Him as our Father than just as the lofty One in heaven who answers our prayers. Once we are convinced He is above all else our Father, who is wholly trustworthy in character, it will be difficult for us to ever question or doubt His wisdom and mercy in what He does. The lady, who claimed she had prayed "all these years", had seemingly missed the privilege of knowing who He "chiefly" is.

We can be sure the records in heaven include many similar incidents we will know nothing about, until God chooses to reveal them to us. But let us consider another incident.

A young service man named Brad was hitch-hiking when picked up by a real-estate broker, Lew Masters. As they rode along, Brad led this business man to receive Christ as his Savior. Out of much appreciation, the older man gave Brad his card as they were about to part, urging him to look him up if he was ever in the Chicago area.

Five years passed before Brad had opportunity to visit Chicago and accept the invitation. And this was his amazing discovery: only a few minutes after they had parted that day, Lew Masters had been killed in an auto accident.

Now, you can hardly imagine Mrs. Masters' joy when she heard from Brad how her husband had received Christ as his Savior just before his death. She said, "I had walked with Christ for many years and had prayed for my husband often. When he was killed, I thought God had not answered my prayers. Now for five years I've been out of fellowship with God—all because I thought He had failed me."[2] That day she was rescued from her bitterness and restored to fellowship.

We must repeat again: how utterly wrong it is to assume our prayers have not been answered. We do not know the whole story.

God alone knows every last chapter, and sometimes chooses to reveal its contents in His own timing... but when He doesn't...!

Perhaps He is pressing us to something more, something much better than just knowing Him as our "Prayer Answerer." From the beginning God's intention was to uniquely design us for fellowship with Himself. Listen! This is no small thing! *Life's ultimate privilege is that through fellowship we can come to know God intimately.* To truly know Who He is—is much better than receiving something from Him. As we have pictured in the diagram, God is ever pressing us to enjoy the larger box.

HOW BIG IS YOUR BOX?

(4) Partnership in

(3) Participation in

His Ways

(2) Communion—

His Purposes

| (1)
Appointment
with God
Jn. 1:3 | Knowing
God
Phil. 2:1
Gen. 18:17 | Eph. 3:9-11
Rom. 8:28 | Phil. 3:10
1 Cor. 3:9 |

It is not God's desire to leave us in the small box. Of course it is proper that we come to our Father with daily petitions and expect to receive answers. Yet to continue this for a lifetime and never press on to intimate communion in knowing Him, His purposes and His ways, would be most tragic.

So our Father will not allow us to remain in the smaller box; He will press us on to a participation in His purposes, and even beyond to the largest box where we become partners with Him in all His ways. WHAT AN INVITATION!

> ... to meet Him daily and share our needs and concerns,
> ... to intimately know HIM, Who He chiefly is,
> ... to participate with Him in His eternal purpose,
> ... to become partners with Him in all His ways.

HOW BIG IS YOUR BOX? If you have determined to remain in the first small box, you have surely resisted the Father's pressing you on to new fellowship. Oh Lord, AWAKEN OUR HEARTS to appreciate our high calling. Imagine! We are invited to partnership with the God of the universe. What a privilege! To better understand this is the object of our 15 day journey together.

In one of our earlier books, THE ULTIMATE INTENTION, we have explained that God is, above all else, the Eternal Father who has purposed for Himself, a vast family of sons conformed to the image of our Lord Jesus. Since our Father God is Himself dedicated to realizing this eternal purpose, we also are invited to participate with Him in fulfilling this glorious purpose. Yet many who have recognized this revelation of His paternal purpose, must now press on to discover and embrace the splendor of His ways. Therefore our concern in these lessons is not only with the *what:* God's paternal purpose, but also with the *how:* OUR PARTNERSHIP IN HIS WAYS of fulfilling it.

Watchman Nee has written, ". . . when anyone through revelation really comes to see that God is God and that man is man, he can do no other than bow down and worship. . . . It is necessary to go a step further. . . to also *adore His ways.* We bow before Him in adoration for what He is in Himself, and we also accept with adoration all the ways He chooses to lead us and all the things it pleases Him to bring into our lives. We must learn to walk step by step; and if we walk before God we shall learn to *adore His ways.* Spiritually our entire future hinges on the matter of our worshipful acceptance of all His dealings with us."[3]

DISCOVERING AND EMBRACING HIS WAYS will require a lifetime. But especially in our praying we will need to understand and embrace His ways. Through increasing fellowship with Him we will more fully appreciate why He will say:

NO! or GROW! or SLOW! or GO!

Yes, we must see, perhaps patiently, how these four answers will increase our fellowship and press us into the larger box.

When God says an emphatic NO! it is usually because He has something different for us than what we have asked. A little boy begged his father to bring a bag of candy when he returned from a shopping trip, but instead he brought him a new bicycle. The apostle Paul asked the Lord to remove the thorn that was vexing him, but the Lord had something better. We recall how Paul prayed three times for this thorn to be removed. "And the Lord said. . . My grace is sufficient for thee: for my strength is made perfect in weakness" (2 Cor. 12:7-10). The Lord was telling Paul, "No, I am not going to remove the thorn, but I will give you sufficient grace so you can endure this thorn."

Was this not better? It might have taken some time for Paul to agree with this. Paul, like many today, wanted *deliverance* but he received *sufficient grace*. God was not about to remove this tool He was using to keep Paul in check; instead He was offering him a greater measure of grace. How much better! Through this intimate fellowship, Paul was discovering another facet in God's character: *He is the All-Sufficient One.* And what is important, is that, while learning to know God, Paul himself is developing character.

When God says we must first GROW, it is because our Father insists on maturity. Consider again both women in the stories at the beginning of our lesson. Actually, God's own character was at stake when they doubted that a loving Father would answer their earnest pleas. Each one claimed she had "prayed long without an answer". Only God knows! It is not for us to judge their praying; let us be encouraged that even the most feeble efforts at praying receive God's full attention. He is a loving Father who bends His ear to the lisping of even the weakest and most uncertain cry of our lips.

Yet God is full of wisdom. There are those times when He is pressing us to move out of our "small box" mentality to His "larger box". Then we are forced to face this question: which should be more important...

getting our prayers answered or

getting to know the Lord?

For our Father to immediately answer our every prayer and leave His child in ignorance and immaturity is unthinkable. Can we imagine God allowing His child to approach the throne of grace, to dial in all the right information—such as praying in His name, for His glory, in faith, etc.—and then to immediately pick up the answer to his prayer? What a privilege! NO! What a come-short of all that God really intends. We must be encouraged that it is always right to expect prayer to be answered, yet it is also imperative that through much diligence and perseverance we come to know God.

I am quite convinced that it would be impossible to "pray all your life" and still not know God as a loving Father, whose wisdom can be trusted, whose promises can be proved as utterly true! Yet when He answers that we must GROW some more, it is because He must enlarge our vision to see as He sees.

Sometimes God says SLOW, which means there may be many others involved, and He will not violate the integrity of their own wills. So this means waiting; which is still another way in which we can grow and come to know the Lord. Consider George Mueller, the man of prayer to whom all the nations look with such admiration. James Mc Conkey tells how Mueller had patiently prayed for five personal friends. After five years one came to Christ. In ten more years two more were saved. He prayed on for twenty-five years before the fourth man was saved. Until the time of Mueller's death, he had prayed for the fifth man almost fifty-two years. This man came to Christ a few months later.

Another friend, A.T. Pierson, asked Mueller a short time before he died, if he had asked anything of God that had not been granted. Mueller explained how he had prayed sixty-two years for two men to be converted, and neither of them had showed any signs of that happening. Then he was asked, "Do you expect God to convert them?"

"Certainly! Do you suppose that God would put upon His child for sixty-two years the burden of two souls if He had no purpose of their conversion?"

Shortly after this conversation, Mueller died. Dr. Pierson continues, "While preaching in his pulpit in Bristol, I referred to this. As I was going out, a lady said to me, 'One of those men was my uncle, and he was converted and died a few weeks ago. The other man was brought to Christ in Dublin. . . I understand.' "

CONSIDER GEORGE MUELLER'S FIVE REASONS why he believed his prayers for the unsaved must be answered:

1. I have had no shadow of doubt in praying for their salvation, knowing as I do that it is the Lord's will that they should be saved, for He "would have all men to be saved, and to come unto the knowledge of the truth" (1 Tim.2:4). "And this is the confidence that we have in Him that if we ask anything according to His will, He heareth us" (1 Jn.5:14).

2. I have never pleaded for their salvation in my own name, but in the all-worthy name of my precious Lord Jesus (Jn.14:14), that is, on the ground of His merit and worthiness, and on that alone.

3. I have (always) believed in the ability and willingness of God to answer my prayers (Mk.11:24).

4. I have not allowed myself (to continue) in known sin, for, "If I regard iniquity in my heart, the Lord will not hear me" (Ps.66:18).

5. I have continued in believing prayer for over fifty two years, and shall so continue until the answer is given. "Shall not God avenge His own elect, which cry day and night unto Him?" (Lk.18:7)

Then it becomes clear! God does answer prayer. Yes, not according to our whims, but His wisdom. Only through increasing fellowship with Him in His ways, can we joyfully embrace His NO! GROW! SLOW! or GO!

How much all of us are like little children who need the careful nurturing of our loving Father. How often I have personally thanked my Father, that He has not answered some of my prayers. At the time I was so convinced it was right, so right—that I should "command Him according to the works of His own hands" (Isa.45:11). But He simply replied, "You need to grow some more!"

How well Theodore Monod illustrates this. He was telling a little friend about Jesus healing blind Bartimaeus. "And what," said he to the little boy, "would you have asked from Jesus if you had been blind?"

"Oh," said the child, with a glowing face and kindling eyes, "I should have asked Him for a nice little dog with a collar and chain to lead me about." Yes, too often like little children we ask for a seeing-eye dog instead of for eyes to see. And then we wonder why our Lord might say, NO, I have something better; or He might say, when you GROW you may want to change your request. Then again, He may say, SLOW, for I am getting some valuable work done in you and others while you patiently wait.

And best of all, sometimes God says "GO!" which means that He is ready to supply what we ask, and then as we take each new step in confidence—we can receive.

QUICKENING THROUGH GOD'S WORD

Finally, we understand why so many, who have preceded us in the race, have been gripped by this glorious privilege of coming to intimately know God through fellowship.

Paul wrote to the believers at Phillipi, "That I might KNOW HIM ..." (Phil.3:10).

John said, "And this is life eternal, that they might KNOW THEE the only true God, and Jesus Christ, whom thou hast sent" (Jn.17:3).

Daniel prophesied, "But the people that do KNOW THEIR GOD shall be strong and do exploits" (Dan.11:32).

Jeremiah warned, "Let not the wise man glory in his wisdom... but let him that glorieth glory in this, that he understandeth and KNOWETH ME, that I am the Lord..." (Jer.9:23).

David expressed this same longing in different words, "One thing have I desired of the Lord, that will I seek after that I may dwell... behold... enquire.... When thou saidst, Seek ye my face, my heart said unto thee, THY FACE LORD WILL I SEEK." David longed to know Him—the One he had enjoyed during so many hours of intimate fellowship. (Ps.27:4)

There are many others in Your Book who had this one passion: TO KNOW YOU MORE FULLY.

Henceforth, this same passion shall be mine!

AURAKEN MY HEART. . . with a new longing to KNOW You!

FATHER, I do acknowledge how often I have judged You according to my limited knowledge of what seemed best. I now can rest! You have not yet published the last chapter in every story, even though it has happened. Forgive me for my hasty, judgmental spirit, when I doubted Your wisdom or doubted that You even cared. Henceforth I shall confess Your faithfulness. All that I do know of You and of Your ways causes me to announce boldly that You are worthy; You are right even though I do not fully comprehend. Father, it is good to know that Your wisdom transcends the wisdom of men, and that You are wholly trustworthy and consistent in Your character.

What new encouragement! Now with new diligence I will pray for certain members of my own family who yet seem so indifferent to Your claims on their lives. If George Mueller could pray all those years, I will not faint, nor question Your wisdom. Help me to really know Your voice and to recognize when You are saying no, grow, slow, or go. I am more confident now, knowing that You have surely answered some requests I will not know about until that day in Eternity. But even more, Lord, I do want to live in the "largest box" where I am so one-with-You, that I become a partner in Your blessed ways. Even if it means much more stretching as I wait and persevere, it will be worthwhile. For above all else, I know that I am coming to KNOW YOU. Your ways are beyond finding out. How great You are! Even when I do not understand Your ways, I love You! Amen!

OVERFLOWING GRATITUDE:

How my heart wants to sing with Paul, as he exults in his exhortation to Timothy: "I KNOW WHOM (not what) I have believed. . . ." Yes, Paul—what ultimate privilege! And what has now just begun will continue throughout the ages! Glory! (Sing it with me).

> But I know whom I have believed,
>   And am persuaded that He is able
> To keep that which I've committed
>   Unto Him against that day.
>
> I know now why God's wondrous grace
>   To me He hath made known,
> And why unworthy—Christ in love
>   Redeemed me for His own.
>
> I know not how the Spirit moves,
>   Convincing men of sin,
> Revealing Jesus thro' the Word,
>   Creating faith in Him.
>   (James McGranahan)

PRAYER REQUESTS   DATE ANSWERED

_____
_____
_____
_____
_____
_____
_____
_____
_____
_____
_____
_____
_____
_____
_____
_____
_____
_____
_____

DAY THREE

AS YOU COME to your time of daily fellowship, I hope you are getting alone—that is, away from the distractions, away from others who might hinder or limit your intimacy with God. Most of us have discovered that the best time is early in the morning when we are still fresh and free from pre-occupations.

Be practical! If you are a night person that may be the best time for you. Whatever—be determined and diligent to keep the same time every day. Remember, there may be a dozen urgent things pressing for immediate attention, but the all-important thing is GETTING HELP FROM GOD for discerning what things are of eternal value.

It could be you are facing some seemingly impossible situations this very day? God may have allowed this in order to get your attention. Your utter bankrupty has prepared you for recognizing the importance of YOUR HELPER.

OUR LESSON TODAY uncovers a prevailing weakness among large numbers of God's children:

> Many who realize that the Holy Spirit indwells every believer, have not, as yet, recognized the ways in which they can cooperate with their blessed Helper.

Others have written about the Holy Spirit's working in effective prayer fellowship, so we will just summarize a few of the important ways in which we can cooperate with our Helper.

THIS FIRST STORY told by Wentworth Pike, an instructor at Prairie Bible Institute, encourages us to honor and expect more of the Holy Spirit's dealings with us in our prayer-fellowship.

The Importance of our Helper

PASTOR WENTWORTH PIKE tells about going into a room of the church to pray for the Sunday evening service:

As I prayed, a strong compulsion came into my heart to pray for a person to be saved in the service. Furthermore, I felt that the prayer should not be merely that some person would be saved, but that there was a particular person for whom that request should be made. . . I did not know who the person was. I tried to dismiss the impression as the working of my imagination, but I could not. My head reasoned: If God desired that I pray for a particular person to be saved, would He not indentify the person? My heart simply said, "Pray."

"Who is it, Lord?" I asked. No voice came in answer, no handwriting on the wall, no vision. Yet the compulsion remained unabated—not a dark, depressive cloud, but a convincing conviction.

I prayed for first one and then another unsaved person in the community but with the feeling that those prayers were not given by the Spirit, and the compulsion did not dissipate. The voice within was as clear as an audible voice would have been: "No, I have one particular soul for you to intercede for, one that I want to save in the service tonight!"

It was incredible. Nothing like this had ever happened to me before. I was not given to dreams or visions or voices and did not expect any now. Nor did I have any; only that persistent inner conviction. I thought that perhaps I had been working too hard and my imagination was working overtime, so I went for a walk. By the time I returned from my rather lengthy stroll the inner conviction was stronger than ever. So I prayed something like this. "Lord, I believe there is one particular unsaved soul which You want to bring to Yourself in tonight's service. I don't know who it is. . . but save this soul tonight. Bring him or her under deep conviction. . . ." I don't remember now all that I said. I probably prayed against Satan, resisted him in Jesus' name, asked the Lord to remove the veil Satan had put on the eyes of the unidentified person so the light of the Gospel could shine in. While I have forgotten the exact words, I don't think I'll ever forget that afternoon.

When the time came for some men to meet with me for prayer the hour before the evening service, I wondered whether I should tell them about the strange burden. Would they think I was a bit queer.

But I soon found myself blurting it out. They did not react negatively, but prayed in this vein:

"Lord, You know who this person is You have laid on our pastor's heart. Save him tonight, Lord."

Getting up from my knees, I then walked down the hall to the sanctuary. As I walked through the doorway near the platform, a man and a little girl came through the main entrance. He looked around as though uncertain whether to proceed.

"Good evening, I'm Wentworth Pike, the pastor," I greeted him and extended my hand.

"Can I join your church?" he asked with no introduction. All over his face was written "troubled soul." I had never seen him before.

"Well, I'm not sure that joining the church is what you need." I replied. "Let's sit over here for a few minutes and get acquainted until time for the service to begin."

"I don't know what it is I need," he exclaimed, "but I've got to get right with God."

As the people were arriving for the service, the conversation continued, and the visitor's need for salvation came into sharper focus.

When it was time for the service to begin, I encouraged him to listen carefully to the message, which would present the plan of salvation, and to come foward when the invitation was given to receive the Lord Jesus Christ as Savior.

He responded immediately to the invitation. After personal counselling and prayer, he stood before the congregation, smiling through his tears, and told this fascinating story.

"About two o'clock this afternoon a strange thing happened.

My little girl and I were at home alone. I was reading the Sunday comics to her when the strangest feeling came over me. I just knew that I had to get right with God. I put the paper down and said, 'Come on, Honey, let's go for a ride.' "

"I didn't know where to go for help. The only place I could think of was a little church out in the community where I went a few times when I was a boy. When we got there, the grass in the yard was knee high and there were boards on the windows. Just then a man came down the road and I asked him whether there would be a service there tonight. 'No,' he said, 'that church has been closed for ten years.'

"So we just got back in the car and drove around, but I couldn't get rid of the feeling that I had to get right with God. As I drove back into town, I came down this street (I never had driven through this part of town before) and noticed the sign out in front of your church. Somehow, I just knew that this was the place where I was going to find the answer. When I came in, the pastor talked to me and showed me from the Bible that what I needed was to be saved. His sermon made it all so plain, so I received Jesus as my Savior and that awful feeling I had all afternoon is gone."

I glanced around at those men who had prayed with me before the service. Some were grinning, while others were wiping tears from their eyes.[1]

WHO CAN EXPLAIN THIS GRACIOUS WORKING OF THE HOLY SPIRIT?

The apostle Paul surely understood what pastor Pike experienced, for he exhorts us that there are those times when. . .

"... we know not how to pray as we ought. . .
... but the Spirit helps us in our weakness. . .
... the Spirit Himself intercedes with sighs too
    deep for words" (Rom. 8:26 RSV).

An English evangelist further illustrates this working of our indwelling Helper in this amazing incident:

A great many years ago a poor widow woman was being pressed by a store-keeper to pay an account which she knew she had already settled.

In that case, he demanded that she produce a receipt. Quite certain she had received one, she hunted and hunted, but was unable to find it. Desperately she searched through the piles of papers and letters, but to no avail—the receipt was not to be found.

Finally, the day arrived when the store-keeper would wait no longer. He came to her house with an angry demand for her immediate payment, or she would be cast into a debtor's prison.

In that moment of distress she turned her heart to the Lord. Hopeless, helpless, inwardly groaning, she cried out, "Lord, You alone are my Helper!" She did not know how to pray, or what words could express the deepest groaning in her spirit. But the "deep" within her was calling to the "Deep" in God.

In that very moment, a butterfly flew into the room through an open window. Her little boy, eager to catch the beautiful creature, ran after it. The frightened insect flew over to the wall and dropped down behind a trunk. In his eagerness to catch it, the boy pushed out the trunk.

There it was! Behind the trunk, on the floor, lay the missing receipt! Snatching it up excitedly, the poor widow showed it to the store-keeper who went away disgruntled. His own handwriting proved the debt had been paid.

It was indeed the groaning Spirit interceding within her spirit that had brought the answer. Nature responded with a butterfly, but it was the God of nature who directed the butterfly.

> Sometimes He works in a very spectacular
> manner as He uses a butterfly;
> But more often He is the God who delights to
> "hide Himself" in the midst of nature.
>
> Sometimes He works by an inner compulsion
> so strong—as Pastor Pike experienced;
> But more often He pulls so gently at our heart, we
> must be very sensitive to even recognize His wooing.

It is to be expected that doubters will seek to explain away any personal involvement by God; even those of us who have been born of the Spirit need to become more open to God's intervening in our lives. Actually we are privileged to have two Helpers: our Lord Jesus is seated above acting as our heavenly Helper, but we also have God's Spirit indwelling our spirit acting as our personal Helper. Yet it is alarming! Even among those who claim to know much about the Holy Spirit's working, there is such a slowness to really cooperate with Him.

LET US NOW CONSIDER SOME PRACTICAL WAYS OUR HELPER waits to assist us from day to day:

Our Helper prays through us. Sometimes we come up against a blank wall in our praying. The situation is so complicated and confusing that we are bewildered as to how we should pray. What should we request? What is best for all concerned? What will bring glory to God? It is in such moments of desperation, like the widow woman, that we cry out. We may not realize what we are doing, yet as our spirit groans for help, God's Spirit is working within our spirit—inwardly groaning according to God's will. It is like a burden that cannot reach our mental consciousness for expression.

Surely this is what we have seen in both pastor Pike and the widow woman. That wordless cry in our spirit, when joined with God's Spirit, is more powerful than the most wonderful outpouring of words in beautiful expression. Yes, there are those times when our spirit can only "sigh" or "groan." We need to turn to our indwelling Helper who carries our deepest longing to the throne above and presents the need to God.

Our Helper directs us according to God's will. I'm sure with all of us there are those times when we think we know His will only to later discover how wrong we were. Not only were we ignorant, but sometimes even our heart-motive was not right. Then it is the Holy Spirit who brings us into His "light" so that our heart-desire is adjusted, and we are ready for the glory of God at any cost.

Our Helper exposes the vain analyzings of our mind. During those days prior to her amazing recovery of the receipt, we do not know how the poor widow woman had been praying. Yet any of us who know the "analyzings" of our own mind know what it is to lie restless through the night, analyzing our problems. We lie there pondering, searching, fruitlessly analyzing. Our thoughts go like this: If only I hadn't been so careless with the receipt; if only I could learn to be more orderly with important things; if only my husband had not left me alone with so much responsibility; if only that store-keeper would show more mercy; if only I could get a job that would help pay the bills. . . if only. . . if only. . . if only! What fruitless reasonings!

Or perhaps you recognize that little "what if", which is just another analyzing: What if that man really forecloses, and I lose my home? What if I get sick and can't take care of my son? . . . what if. . . what if? Oh, the endless turmoil of reasonings. Do you not recognize this tyranny of an analyzing mind? Our Helper is available, waiting to expose these vain frustrations of our mind.

I emphasize this because there are so many "victims" who cannot pray as they ought until they learn to cast down these fruitless reasonings of their mind. Indeed we cannot expect much help from our Helper until we recognize and then reject these as fruitless activity of our analyzing mind. Effective praying is coming into God's light, not the dim light of our own mental reasonings.

Our Helper will restrain us in the abundance of words. Someone has well said, "It is time to quit sending all that junk mail up to God." Only as we learn to hold every request before Him (i.e. "in His light") can we sense whether our asking is according to His mind and will. This is why we so desperately need our Helper: "In Thy light shall we see light. . ."(Ps. 36:4). He is the only One who can keep all things in God's light.

What folly! So much praying in beautiful phrases and well-worn expressions is simply prayer chatter. We all have been guilty! Our hope is that as we are restrained in our abundance of empty words, we shall learn to pray more definitely according to the heart of God.

Our Helper imparts holy desire. In his book G.H.C. Macgregor asks, "And after we have been brought to a point where we must pray or die, after we have been brought to a condition of soul which makes it absolutely necessary that we should get to God in prayer, who but the Holy Spirit can help us to pray as we ought? Who but He can fill us with intense desire? Who but He, in the midst of our modern busy life, can still and quiet the soul before God? Who but He can give us the sweet simplicity of childhood as He leads us to the Father's presence? Who but He can give us the boldness which takes no refusal, and obtains the blessing?"[2]

Our Helper will enable us to effectively stand against wickedness. What shall we pray against, or whom shall we pray against? Not against flesh or blood, nor against men and women, but against the prince of the air, the god of this world, and all his plans and schemes. We need to be very clear in this, and know how to stand "in the Spirit" against Enemy interference.

An example: One Christian sister had no choice but to be in a class that day, even though it was an uncomfortable situation. She knew of no other Christian there, and from her quick observation it seemed likely that many were involved in drugs, drink and a cycle of immorality that enslaves. The most difficult thing about the oppressive situation was the foul language of the professor. The profanity that flowed from his mouth was very repulsive to her as a Christian. One part of her alert mind listened to the instruction, but quietly within her spirit she began to resist and to bind the evil spirit behind the profanity. At first there was no change, but she persisted. By lunch time that spirit had been bound. Not one word of profanity was uttered by the professor during the afternoon session. Only the help of the Holy Spirit could enable her to maintain this faith-position.

Consider another: An elderly saint had become a bed patient. Her normally cooperative spirit, strangely, began to give way to rebellion and anger. Alert Christian nurses quickly recognized that evil spirits were taking advantage of a weakened body and mind. Binding the enemy spirits and pleading the blood of Jesus brought release to the troubled patient. Soon a sweet, cooperative spirit again was in full control.

Another example: A neighbor's unreasonably loud, worldly music was most distracting to a Christian lady who sat reading her Bible. This blaring music not only bothered her but the entire neighborhood, and was most annoying as she knelt to pray. She took dominion in Jesus' name and commanded that music to cease. Within a minute the blaring music which had been playing for some time was suddenly shut off, and her prayer time could proceed without distraction. She was learning to cooperate with her Helper!

Our Helper will deal with habits that do not honor Christ.

For years a woman had been struggling to stop smoking. As a child of the King she felt convicted about being in bondage to some tobacco leaves wrapped in a paper. Yet she felt helpless to get free of this, and was living in discouragement—condemned. Then one night in a short dream she saw the face of a speaker at a recent meeting who had mentioned the smoking problem. Immediately a hand and arm with a lighted cigarette between the fingers came into view. In the dream the fingers began vigorously tamping out the cigarette. The dream ended with that picture.

The next morning the dream was still vividly pressing her attention. She wondered if its meaning could be as obvious as it seemed. Pondering this, she automatically reached for her cigarettes. A single one was left in the package. Upon lighting it she soon found that it tasted so different—in fact not at all good. With much disgust she tamped the cigarette out exactly as in the dream. From that hour she has had no appetite to smoke. What happened? Inwardly her will was standing with God against this slavery she hated; thus her Helper was free to break the outward shackles—her habit was gone. Thank God! All His children have this same indwelling Helper, who waits to deliver from any habit that dishonors the Lord.

Our Helper comes to reveal those things that God has deliberately hidden from the natural mind. No doubt you have had this happen: As you were reading some portion of God's Word, suddenly new meaning "jumped out of a verse." It was as though your dim flashlight turned into a vast torchlight helping you to "see" more than natural eye ever saw before. What you saw was not new, just new to you!

This revealing work of the Holy Spirit should not be unusual. God has intended that all the vast treasures He has stored up "in heavenly places" should become available to His children. But many have not "seen" because God's Spirit must reveal this to them.

For example, in the ways of this world a parent usually must die before a child receives his inheritance. But in the spiritual life Christ's death that brought us our inheritance took place two thousand years ago at Calvary. Our spiritual inheritance is available NOW.

It is the revealing work of the Spirit to help us see this fact. Actually once we see, it altogether changes our prayer life. No longer is there any need of pleading with God to change undesirable circumstances or to grant us something we need. No, the Revealer must simply show us what has already been done—stored up for us. Thus our primary petition should be for revelation so as to open our eyes to see all that God has stored up for us in Christ.

Let me repeat, there is such a change when this revealing work of our Helper uncovers what God has already done. Suddenly our praying is not to shift or change some outward circumstance, but for a revelation of how God is already working. Yes, our prayer then turns to active waiting on Him for that insight.

To this very point Catherine Marshall writes, "When the insight comes, then faith—'the substance of things not seen'—follows as surely as the sun rises each morning. This 'knowing' is altogether different from all pull-yourself-up-by-your-own-bootstraps faith techniques. How often I have tried to quell my own doubts by rebuking negativism and concentrating on the positive—and have tried to call that faith. Yet all such self-help gimmicks are light years away from Jesus' quiet knowing that wrought mighty miracles."[3]

Thank God! One solid experience of our Helper's revealing work is worth more than a dozen years of struggling to uncover the ways of God. Believe me, I have found it so.

FINALLY, SOME CONCLUSIONS ABOUT OUR HELPER.

- Not enough of God's children today appear to really believe that the Holy Spirit is waiting and willing to do for them all that Jesus would do if He were on earth. Consequently many in their personal lives, and many in churches are operating without true dependence upon the Holy Spirit. Therefore we see much substituting of "toys and trifles" in the place of the Spirit.

- It is not enough to admit that the Holy Spirit is present in fellowship meetings; there is also a great need for "honoring His Person" and submitting to His executive work of guiding each meeting.

- It is not proper to beg God for more of the Holy Spirit; simply set your heart to exalt and glorify the Lord Jesus, and the Helper will mightily manifest His special concern for turning the spotlight on our lovely Lord Jesus.

- It is not honoring Him to acknowledge that he is merely the Spirit of Truth and thereby lock Him into the cold pages of Scripture. As A.W. Tozer insists, "He has individuality, will and intelligence; He can hear, speak, desire, grieve and rejoice; He can be quenched, silenced and wounded... He can penetrate your personality and your own spirit." [4] He has come to complete His work in each individual and in the corporate body of Christ as He is rightly honored.

QUICKENING FROM YOUR WORD.

From among the abundance of Scripture verses, let me select these four that explain the Holy Spirit's helping work. He is . . .

OUR COUNSELOR: "... if I go away... the Counselor will come to you..." Jn.16:7 RSV.

OUR ENERGIZER: "...but ye shall receive power when the Holy Spirit has come UPON you" Acts 1:8 RSV.

OUR COMFORTER: "... and I will pray the Father, and He shall send you another Comforter" Jn.14:16 KJV.

OUR TEACHER: "... But the Counselor, the Holy Spirit will teach you ..." Jn.14:26.

<u>Awaken My Heart</u>. . . Lord, to really appreciate my indwelling Helper.

For many years I have known that He comes to indwell each one as we are born into God's family, but He is more than a Presence who abides. He is more than a Guest who resides in His own temple, which we are. He is the God of the universe who dwells in our humanity, and He has come to assume the lowly position of HELP-ER. *It seems hard to grasp! This Royal Guest has come as our Helper. Oh, Father it is too much for me to comprehend such privilege of fellowship with You—through the Spirit. (Phil.2:1)*

Father, I know it will be impossible for me to run life's race triumphantly. But I now see that You have made this possible, for Your Holy Helper has come to run along-side. I am without excuse!

<u>Overflowing Gratitude</u>.   You can sing this to the more familiar tune, "Sun of My Soul".

> O Breath of God, breathe on us now,
> And move within us while we pray;
> The spring of our new life art Thou,
> The very light of our new day.
>
> O strangely art Thou with us, Lord,
> Neither in height or depth to seek;
> In nearness shall Thy voice be heard;
> Spirit to spirit Thou dost speak.
>
> Christ is our Advocate on high;
> Thou art our Advocate within;
> O plead the truth, and make reply
> To every argument of sin.
>
> Be with me when no other friend
> Thy mystery of my heart can share;
> And be Thou known, when fears transcend,
> By Thy best name of Comforter.
> (A.H. Vine)

PRAYER REQUESTS   DATE ANSWERED

_____
_____
_____
_____
_____
_____
_____
_____
_____
_____
_____
_____
_____
_____
_____
_____
_____
_____
_____

INSIGHTS FROM LESSON

_____
_____
_____
_____
_____
_____
_____
_____
_____
_____
_____
_____
_____
_____
_____
_____
_____
_____
_____
_____

DAY FOUR

HOW GOES THE JOURNEY? As we get better acquainted with God, we recognize that He is above all—our Father: One who is greatly concerned and available to help us in our deepest needs. Once He seemed far, far away in the distant heavens, but now, because of the rescue work of our Lord Jesus, we can approach Him as His children. Therefore we have come to better understand WHO WE ARE, because we know WHO HE IS. What a privilege!

There are those times in our walk with the Lord, when we sense such a lack of understanding, of confidence, of direction, of faith—we seem to be stalled in our "race." As we shall see, this is our opportunity to cast ourselves upon Him for His great mercy.

TODAY, we consider this question:

What is the difference between the prayer for mercy and the prayer of faith?

Could it be when God hears our simple plea for help, that more often He responds according to His mercy, than to our faith? In coming to know God more intimately as Father, we discover He is both merciful and righteous. Often when we have little faith, we can only plead for His mercy, yet at other times we have a measure of faith to ask Him to be righteous in fulfilling His Word. Today, we shall primarily consider the value and validity of the MERCY PRAYER.

HELEN ROSEVEARE, faithful veteran of missionary service, demonstrates her sacrificial work among orphan children in Africa. Those who know the mature faith of this missionary doctor, realize how often she must have been pressed to the Lord for His provision. Let us read her story.

A Time for the Mercy Prayer

DR. HELEN ROSEVEARE was called out one night to a maternity case. In spite of all she and the nurses could do, the mother died, leaving a tiny premature baby and a little two-year old girl. In a remote, little hospital in Zaire, the missionary doctor felt such utter helplessness.

She spoke to the midwives. "Our problem in keeping this baby alive is to maintain a steady temperature."

There was no incubator, no electricity! A nurse went out to get a box to put the baby in and some cotton wool to wrap it in. Another midwife went to fill the hot-water bottle. Another stoked the fire.

"I'm awfully sorry, Doctor," said the one on the hot-water bottle detail. "I boiled the water and poured it in and—buh! The bottle burst. And it's the last hot-water bottle we have."

There was no drug store where they could buy one, so the doctor said, "All right, put the baby as near the fire as you can. You must sleep between the baby and the door. Your job is to protect the little one from any drafts."

The next day at midday Dr. Roseveare gathered her group of orphan children around her for prayer as she did everyday. She gave them various things to pray for and told them of the premature baby and how difficult it was going to be to keep the little one alive. She mentioned the burst hot-water bottle and told them of the two-year old who was crying because her Mommie had died.

During the prayer time one of the children, a ten-year-old girl named Nammy, took the matter up in prayer in the usual very blunt way that African youngsters do, "Please, God, send us a hot-water bottle—be no good tomorrow, God, the baby'll be dead. Please send it this afternoon." And then she added, "And while You're about it, God, would You send a doll for the little girl so she'll know You still love her?"

Could the missionary really say, "Amen"? She didn't honestly believe that God could do it. Oh, of course she knew that God could do anything. Hadn't she sung it many times and heard it preached? Was it really possible that He could cope with this one?

In the three years she had been there, she had never received a parcel. They just didn't come. Mail arrived only now and then when someone happened to be traveling in the right direction. And if anyone in her homeland of Great Britain should send a parcel, who would put in a hot-water bottle? She was on the equator!

"Well, about midway through the afternoon," she relates, "I was teaching in the nurses' training school when somebody came saying, 'There's a car outside your house, Doctor.' I went across, but when I got there, the car had gone. There on the veranda was a large box all the way from the United Kingdom! I think I felt the tears then. I felt I couldn't open it alone. I sent for the orphan kiddies, and we opened it together. On the top there were lots of bright vests that they love. Their eyes lit up as I threw them out, praying all the while, 'Please, God, there must be enough vests to go around.' Then I came to some knitted bandages for the leprosy patients, and the children looked a bit bored. Next, I uncovered a large bar of soap and they looked more bored. However, their eyes lit up again when I found a nice package of mixed fruit. It would make a batch of cookies for the weekend. And then I pulled it out—the brand new rubber hot-water bottle! I cried."

Nammy was in the front row of the children. She rushed forward saying, "If God sent the bottle, He must have sent a doll." Diving into the parcel with both hands, she pulled out the dollie. Looking up at Dr.Roseveare, she asked, 'Please, Mommie, may I go to that little girl so she'll know that Jesus really loves her?' "

The parcel had been on the way five months. Imagine! Five months before, God had burdened some Sunday school group to put a parcel together. He had urged some teacher to put in a hot-water bottle even though the parcel would be going to the equator; He had caused some child in far-away England to give a doll for a little motherless child in Africa. Yes—God wanted to answer a child's prayer even before it had been expressed.[1]

WAS IT GOD'S MERCY OR NAMMY'S FAITH?

Many speak of the faith of a little child and from an incident such as this would emphasize how much easier it is for a little one to trust God. Perhaps! Could it be that sometimes God hears a simple plea—as with little Nammy—and responds more out of His great mercy than because of her faith? I am sure that we can offer that as a possibility. For it is surely true; as we get older, we become more complicated, and much religious "knowledge" gets in the way of simple faith.

I have often pondered the words of an old prayer-warrior who insisted, "Sometimes God's answering is more out of His mercy than it is because of our faith. It seems in the early stages of our walk with Him, He often responds out of mercy and compassion, because our measure of faith is so very weak or small. Then when it is time for us to grow up and begin to exercise more faith, He will sometimes discontinue showing His mercy."

In the light of this we might call Nammy's a prayer for mercy. It would seem her asking was based more on the sure mercy of God than on any definite promise being claimed.

Recently I discovered that the late Catherine Marshall also refers to a Mercy Prayer. In an INTERCESSORS prayer circular,[2] Catherine relates what happened when her friend, Betty, asked God to be merciful during a very distressing scene one Sunday morning. As two young parents stood before the pastor in front of the church, their baby began not only crying, but screaming at times.

Betty says, "I could see how embarrased those parents were, and I felt such compassion for them. Then the thought dropped into my mind that there was no way I could possibly be feeling more compassion than Jesus was feeling.

"So I simply said, 'Lord Jesus, have mercy on that baby and on that father and mother.' "

"Catherine," she added, "it was remarkable. The crying stopped immediately as if a faucet had been turned off."

Catherine continues, "Since talking with Betty, I've spent several of my morning prayer times asking the Lord for insights about the validity and effectiveness of the Mercy Prayer. Passage after passage of Scripture was brought to my attention. I saw that many of Jesus' healings, as recorded in the Gospels, came as the result of a prayer for mercy by some sufferer.

"For instance, there were the two blind men sitting by the side of the road. Hearing that Jesus was passing by, the two men cried out, 'Have mercy on us, O Lord, thou son of David.' Then there were the ten lepers. Since lepers were ostracized from public gatherings, these ten men stood at a distance crying almost in unison, 'Jesus, have mercy on us.'

"The Master did not question each man about how well he had kept the law or how righteous he was. Out of overflowing compassionate love, He healed all ten on the spot. 'I will have mercy and not sacrifice, for I am not come to call the righteous, but sinners to repentance,' Jesus announced."

IS THERE A SPECIAL TIME TO USE THE MERCY PRAYER?

Because we see God working for little Nammy, answering out of His great mercy, we might assume that we can use this forever, as though appealing to His compassion is all we shall ever need. Hardly! There is nothing wrong with this plea for mercy when we sense we have little or no faith to claim His Word. But appealing to God's mercy is not to be the only kind of prayer we offer to God.

As we progress in our faith journey, it becomes evident that God does not always respond to our plea for mercy; we become perplexed! We wonder why? It is simply that God, as a Father, is concerned for our development. Initially He imparts to all His children a "measure of faith." (Rom.12:3) This is a "faith that receives"—as in accepting what God gives. In those beginning days God was pleased to do things for us; now He wants to develop in us an increasing "proportion of faith" (Rom.12:6) so that He might work through us. This is a "faith that takes"—as in actively pursuing God's will. Yes, our heavenly Father is concerned that we not only understand the Prayer for Mercy, but also exercise the Prayer of Faith.

PRAYER FOR MERCY	PRAYER OF FAITH
God responds to any plea for help because of His compassion	God responds to any claiming of His Word, because He is righteous.
God demonstrates His consistent character, even when we are not aware or are wholly undeserving.	God demonstrates His faithfulness when we appeal to the consistency of His character.
God withholds judgment (for a time) because He is not willing that any should perish.	God is righteous to fulfill His Word as we steadfastly stand for all His purposes.
RECEIVING faith—as in accepting.	TAKING faith—as in pursuing.

The prayer for mercy, as we describe above, is based on God's longsuffering and compassion. We will, no doubt, throughout our entire walk with Him, come to those times when all we can do is plead, "God be merciful." Remember, God is always demonstrating His character even when we are unaware. When He counsels with Abraham about the wickedness of Sodom, God is showing mercy to Lot and his family, not because of them, but because of uncle Abraham's intercession. Thus He stayed the impending hour of judgment until any of the righteous within Sodom could be warned to escape. "Shall not the Judge of all the earth do right?" (Gen.18:25). Here we see God's great mercy toward Lot, but we also see Abraham's prayer of faith as He appeals to the consistency of God's character.

The prayer of faith is for those who are learning how to actively cooperate with God in His purposes. The basis of any request is that we stand on God's Word and His willingness and faithfulness to fulfill it. In this light, the apostle Paul writes of developing an increasing "proportion of faith." (Rom.12:6) In the prophet Elijah we see an exercise of faith that shuts and opens the heavens. In his writing, the apostle James reminds us that ". . . the fervent, effectual prayer of a righteous man availeth much . . ." (Js. 5:14). James is taking us beyond the claim for mercy to the faith that exercises authority. In this instance James reminds us when the elders of the church—men who have maturity to assume governmental authority—pray this prayer of faith, the sick are healed.

Now let us consider an example of God's showing mercy. In a convent just outside Barcelona, Spain, lived a young girl who felt a terrible load of guilt and sin which she couldn't seem to get rid of. She tried everything. She had done penance; she had fasted; she had confessed; she had struggled to believe; she had even been baptized—yet nothing seemed to help relieve her awful sense of guilt.

One night as she walked idly back and forth in her little room, she turned on the radio and heard a program specially prepared for young people—every night in a different language.

That particular night the program was in Spanish, and she heard for the first time in her life that,

> "Jesus paid it all; all to Him I owe;
> Sin had left a crimson stain;
> He washed it white as snow."

Kneeling there in her convent cell, she gave her life to Jesus Christ. Immediately her struggle ended; for the first time she saw what it meant to trust Christ's finished work as God's provision for her sin. A shaft of light had broken through into her troubled heart—a heart that was as prepared soil. God imparted to her a measure of saving faith—a faith that calls out to Him for mercy. It is a receiving faith that accepts His finished work on her behalf.

NOW AN EXAMPLE OF THE PRAYER OF FAITH! Several years ago a missionary in India took into her home five little orphan girls. They were very naughty. She prayed for them. She taught them and labored with them, but it seemed to no avail. One day in desperation she wrote to her blacksmith friend in America, and said: "I wish you would pray for five little girls that I have taken. Whatever I do makes no impression upon them; they remain as naughty as ever."

What do you think that blacksmith did? He did not plead, "Bless Jennie over there; have mercy on those five orphan girls and bring them to Christ," and then forget all about it? No, when his day's work was finished, and everything was ready to close up, he took that letter and went back into his shop and spent the night wrestling in prayer for the salvation of those girls. Through the night he labored, until the prayer of faith could claim victory. In the morning he wrote to his missionary friend. "Do not be discouraged. God has answered for those five girls, and they will be converted."

Something happened the very next morning after he had prayed. The spirit of conviction came upon those five children over in India, and they came to the missionary weeping, "We have been very naughty. We have not listened to what you told us to do. We have told lies and disobeyed you. We have stolen, and we have done many wicked things. We want to belong to the Lord Jesus. Won't you pray for us?"

When the missionary got the letter a month later and counted back, she realized that her girls had turned to the Lord the day after the blacksmith had spent the night in prayer. All five of those girls eventually became Christian workers. Would you agree that we need many more blacksmiths who have learned to intercede at the throne of God, and who know the effectual fervent prayer of faith?

QUICKEN ME THROUGH YOUR WORD

In a new way I begin to realize how often men in the Bible speak of Your mercy:

David leads them all. "I will sing of the mercies of the Lord forever; with my mouth will I make known thy faithfulness to all

generations. For I have said, mercy shall be built up forever . . ."
(Ps.89:1-2).

Moses prayed, "O satisfy us early with thy mercy that we may
rejoice and be glad all our days" (Ps. 90:14).

Jonah explains, ". . . for I knew that thou art a gracious God,
and merciful, slow to anger, and of great kindness . . ." (Jonah.4:2).

Joel warns, "Rend your heart, and not your garments, and
turn unto the Lord your God: for he is gracious and merciful, slow
to anger, and of great kindness . . ." (Joel 2:13).

Paul exhorts, ". . . that the Gentiles might glorify God for His
mercy . . ." (Rom.15:9). Again he writes, ". . . God, who is rich in
mercy . . ." (Eph.2:4).

Peter explains, ". . . according to his abundant mercy hath
begotten us to a lively hope . . ." (1 Pet.1:3).

AWAKEN MY HEART. . . . to appreciate Your mercy.

*Father, I am thankful that I have in a whole new way realized
You are the God of mercy. I want to join all these who have run the
race before me, who have continually extolled Your mercy. When I
consider each of Your servants, I remember how they exercised the
prayer of faith, but I also recall how sometimes in the weakness of
their humanity they could only plead for mercy.*

*Father, it gives me new courage to realize that I, too, in my
times of weakness—when I have such little faith—can plead for Your
mercy.*

*It is beyond my understanding that You should declare, "I will
have mercy on whom I will have mercy . . . ."*

*You do not need to explain why . . . or when . . . or how—You just
show mercy at Your own discretion. Yes, You are my Father, and
the more I know You, the more I appreciate why You cannot now
make all things perfectly clear. I am also convinced that when You
withhold Your mercy, it is because You are wanting me to be enlarged. I'm sure I would be content to plead for mercy in every
situation, but You desire mature sons whose active faith can move
mountains and subdue kingdoms. Yes, I am learning to be a Father-
pleaser; one who through increasing fellowship is learning to participate with You in Your purposes and to embrace all Your ways.*

<u>OVERFLOWING GRATITUDE</u> causes me to sing . . .

> Teach me thy way, O Lord, Teach me Thy way;
>> Thy gracious aid afford, Teach me Thy way.
> Help me to walk aright; More by faith, less by sight;
>> Lead me with heav'nly light, Teach me Thy way.
>
> Long as my life shall last, Teach me Thy way;
>> Where'er my lot be cast, Teach me Thy way.
> Until the race is run, Until the journey's done,
>> Until the crown is won, TEACH ME THY WAY.
>
> (B. Mansell Ramsey)

PRAYER REQUESTS   DATE ANSWERED

_____

_____

_____

_____

_____

_____

_____

_____

_____

_____

_____

INSIGHTS FROM LESSON

_____

_____

_____

_____

_____

_____

_____

_____

_____

_____

DAY FIVE

ANY REAL PROGRESS IN FELLOWSHIP comes in our learning to be quiet . . . to wait before Him. Most of us have been too full of the "hurry spirit". I think there is no exhortation in the Bible so difficult to obey as "be still and know that I am God."

One of the rewards that comes from our learning to wait before Him, is that we learn how to be more definite in our asking. Faber, the songwriter, must have known by personal experience how much floods in to capture our attention, and how easily our mind wanders. He wrote:

> Ah dearest Lord! I cannot pray,
> My fancy is not free;
> Unmannerly distractions come,
> And force my thoughts from Thee.
> The world that looks so dull all day,
> Glows bright on me at prayer
> And plans that ask no thought but then,
> Wake up and meet me there.

TODAY WE CONSIDER the difference . . .

>   . . . between wholesale and retail praying.
>   . . . between natural and spiritual faith.
>   . . . between the root and the fruit.

In this present hour when so many are searching for some new technique or method for getting their prayers answered, we go back to God's age-old promise: "If you abide in Me . . . ye shall ask what you will." We shall discover both the dangers and the rights we have in ASKING DEFINITELY.

More Definite in our Praying

YEARS AGO, the Free Church of Scotland was holding an important meeting in Aberdeen. Worshipers were flocking in from all nearby towns. An aged man, wending his way to the city on foot, was overtaken by a young theological student; the two walked on together. Despite the difference in their ages, they enjoyed much fellowship as they trekked on toward the city.

At noontime they sat down on a grassy slope to eat the lunch each had brought, first giving God thanks for His gracious provision. Afterwards the aged pilgrim suggested that they pray together before continuing their journey. The young theologian was a bit embarrassed, but agreed, intimating that the elder man should pray first.

Addressing God as his Father in all simplicity, the old gentleman poured out his heart in thanksgiving, then uttered three specific requests. First, he reminded the Lord that he was very hard of hearing; therefore he needed a seat near enough to the pulpit so he could get full benefit of the message. Second, he told the Lord that his shoes were badly worn and not fit for the city streets, so he pleaded for a new pair though he had not the money to purchase them. Last of all, he asked for a place to stay for the night, as he knew no one in Aberdeen and did not know where to look for accommodations.

By this time the young theologian's eyes were wide open. He looked upon the old man with mingled disgust and amazement, thinking it a great impertinence to burden Deity with such trivialities.

When his turn came to pray, he delivered himself of an eloquent, carefully composed discourse, which in turn amazed his old companion, who saw in it nothing that indicated a making known any definite needs to God the Father.

Proceeding on their way, the men reached the church just as the people were crowding in, and it became evident that there was no longer even standing room left. The student thought, "Now we shall see what becomes of this presumptuous prayer. He'll see that God has more to do than use His time saving a seat for a poor, old, country man."

However, at that very moment, someone came out and the old man was just able to squeeze inside the door, where he stood with his hand up to his ear trying to hear what was going on.

Just then, it happened that a young lady in the front pew turned and saw him. Calling a sexton, she said, "My father told me to hold our pew for him until time for the sermon, then, if he did not get here, to give it to someone else. Evidently, he has been detained. Will you please go back and bring up that old man who has his hand to his ear, standing just inside the door?" In a few moments he was sitting in the pew directly before the speaker—so petition number one was fully answered!

Now, in Scotland, some folk always kneel for prayer as the minister leads; others reverently rise to their feet. The old man was the kneeling kind, and the young woman always stood. As she looked down, she couldn't help observing the worn shoes on the feet of the kneeling worshiper.

Since her father was a shoe-dealer, she delicately approached the subject of his need for a better pair of shoes. She asked if she might take him to her father's store, though closed for the night, and present him with a pair. Thus petition two was answered!

At the store, the lady inquired where he was to stay for the night. In all simplicity he answered, "I dinna ken yet. My Father has a room for me, but He has not told me where it is." Puzzled for a moment, she exclaimed, "Oh, you mean your Father-God! Well, I believe we have that room for you. We were saving our guest-room for the Rev. ----, but a telegram came this morning saying he could not come, so now you must be our guest!" Thus the third petition was answered!

You can imagine the astonishment of the young theologian the next day when he discovered how definitely the Lord had answered the old man's prayer! Perhaps it is in order for all of us who have read this faith-building story to ask, is there some secret to asking so definitely and receiving so quickly?[1]

PRACTICAL HELPS IN ASKING DEFINITELY

First, it seems evident that for the old man, prayer was no mere act, but a way of life. It would seem he had developed roots in God—that is, he had learned an abiding fellowship that brought him into such intimacy with God that he could ask in simple confidence. Such roots in God—in His Word, His purposes, and His ways do not come quickly or through casual acquaintance.

It seems the cry of many today is "fruit now and roots later." Yet there are no short-cuts to developing root-life. As we picture below, much of the Scripture points first to our developing roots (abiding) and only then can we expect fruits (answers).

	ROOTS	FRUIT
Ps.37:4	Delight thyself also in the Lord. . .	and He shall give thee the desires of thine heart.
Ps.37:5	Trust also in Him. . .	and He shall bring it to pass.
Jn.15:5	He that abideth in me and I in him. . .	the same bringeth forth much fruit, without me ye can do nothing.
Jn.5:7-8	If ye abide in me and my words abide in you. . .	ye shall ask what you will, and it shall be done unto you . . . that ye bear much fruit.

Who can doubt that the old man enjoyed this intimacy, we call root-life, which allowed him to express his very real needs—not mere wishes or desires? Yes, he had confidence! Therefore the One he loved would give him a good seat, a pair of shoes and a place to sleep that night. Somehow, I believe that God was pleased with this definite asking for his needs.

Second, we assume that knowing God's will is necessary before we can pray definitely. And so we seek to know; yet there is something which always precedes knowing God's will. Wentworth Pike explains: "Discovery follows surrender. Without surrender to God's will, one will probably never know what it is. I repeat: the way to pray in the will of God is not to seek to know what His will is and then decide whether to follow it. That is not faith; it is audacity! We must accept God's will—not on the basis of our enjoyment, understanding, or judgment, nor because we have found out what it is and decided in favor of it—but because it is God's will."[2]

Third, there will be no definite praying until faith is born in the heart. Oswald Sanders stresses this fact: ". . . there are two kinds of faith: natural and spiritual. Only born-again Christians possess spiritual faith, which is a gift of God's grace (cf.Eph.2:8)." By natural faith he refers to such matters as believing that the postal authorities will deliver one's letter, or believing in the moral integrity of a businessman. By spiritual faith he is speaking of viewing things through spiritual eyes and perceiving things invisible to the natural eye.

Who can describe this kind of faith that "sees" and then stands with God even when all circumstances seem contrary? It is a faith instilled in the heart by the message of the Lord through His Word. Whether we feel we have faith or not is irrelevant. Spiritual faith is a disciplined act of obedience based on the fact of God's Word, not on the fickleness of feeling.

BEWARE OF WHOLESALE PRAYING!

In his prayer manual, Peter Lord exhorts us to recognize the difference between retail and wholesale praying: "Wholesale praying goes something like this. I love You, Lord; thank You for all things; forgive me all my sins, bless everybody, and give me all I need. In retail praying one is specific. I thank You, Lord, for my son, John; for shoes, for necessary food, for giving me _____."(3)

Does it seem strange that most of us should fall into this habit of dealing in generalities? It is also most revealing! We are not really expecting an answer, nor are we very clear as to our needs, or about our Father's willingness to supply.

Surely our best examples in praying definitely, come from Scripture. In His lesson on prayer, Jesus taught:

Matt.6:11 ". . . give us this day our daily bread . . . . "
Lk.11:5 ". . . friend, lend me three loaves . . . ."
Mk.10:51 ". . . what wilt thou that I should do . . .?"

In this last verse it is meaningful that our Lord Jesus should urge the blind man to be specific. Jesus had been hearing this man's plaintive cry for mercy. We are sure our Lord recognized his blindness and was ready to grant his plea. Yet He wanted to hear from the man's own lips more than a general petition for mercy. Jesus wanted to hear the definite expression of his need to see. Until the blind man speaks this, he is not healed. Could it be that the real issue in faith centers in our asking specifically?

The beloved Andrew Murray, who is perhaps best known for his books on prayer, explains: "Our prayers must not be a vague appeal to His mercy, an indefinite cry for blessing, but the distinct expression of definite need. Not that His loving heart does not understand our cry, or is not ready to hear. But He desires this for our own sakes. Such definite prayer teaches us to know our own needs better. It demands time, and thought, and self-scrutiny to find out what really is our greatest need. It searches us and puts us to the test as to whether our desires are honest and real, such as we are ready to persevere in."

Murray continues: "Definite prayer 'leads us to judge whether our desires are according to God's Word, and whether we really believe that we shall receive the things we ask for. It helps us to wait for the special answer and to mark it when it comes.' "

Down through the years, I have met many whose lives demonstrated their intimacy with God, and there was always fruit as a result of root-life. One such experience still haunts me. I recall, as a very young man, my privilege of praying with a man deeply devoted in intercession. As we got up from our knees, he smiled and placing his loving arm around my shoulder, said, "You'll never know when God answers your prayer!" He saw the startled look on my face and then hastened to explain. "Some day, my son, you'll learn to be more specific instead of so general." Now I have come to realize that being definite in prayer only comes after developing intimacy with Him.

I still remember another choice vessel of the Lord who had spent more than forty years shut away in prayer warfare. While holding a meeting in a Southern city, I was impressed to take the offering given to me the evening before to this elderly woman whom I had just recently met. As I approached her open door and handed her the envelope of bills and change, her first words were, "Oh, thank You Father. The amount is _____!" I looked again at the figure written on the envelope, for I had not remembered the exact amount.

"How did you know the amount?" I asked her, quite puzzled. "Oh, an hour ago the printer delivered some materials, and the bill was _____. I asked my Father for that amount so I could pay it today."

In the years that followed, I learned to know her better. I came to realize that her deep roots in God and in His Word made this kind of expectancy a daily delight. One day I overheard her asking God to provide some new suits for a young minister. In a few weeks he had several. One night as we left a meeting, she prayed: "Lord, I see something very unusual ahead in the road. Help my brother to drive with special caution." An hour later I had to suddenly swerve my car to miss a body lying in the middle of my lane. An Indian had fallen in a drunken stupor as he made his way home.

UNUSUAL! Not for her. She could be very definite with her Lord, for she had many years of experience in knowing both His Word and His ways.

With new understanding I came to appreciate why Jesus insisted, "If you abide in me ... ye shall ask what ye will ...." The Psalmist also had learned this: "Delight thyself also in the Lord ... and He shall give thee the desires of thine heart" (Ps. 37:4).

It is no longer a secret; those who simply want to "name-it and claim-it" need deeper roots if they want to claim fruit. I do thank God for every lesson learned in praying with those who have known God intimately. How often I have been exposed! Rather than claiming too much, I have been ashamed for claiming too little. My vague and pointless praying revealed how shallow my roots were; thus I had little confidence and expectancy.

AND NOW THIS WARNING!

Those who find a good thing, so often attempt to get more mileage for God. If God delights in our being more definite in praying, they assume it is a very real opportunity for God to receive more glory if He is asked to fulfill the "difficult." If they were giving advice to the old Scotsman, they would encourage him to ask for the front-row seat directly before the speaker; to ask for brown, wing-tip, Florsheim, size 10, B width shoes; to ask for a private room on the third floor overlooking the mountains, a bed with a king-size orthopedic mattress. Why not ask largely? Does God not delight in doing the "impossible?" They imagine for God to fulfill such exact requirements would demonstrate His direct intervention and therefore bring glory to Him.

I wonder!

It is possible that on some occasion God may direct someone to such an extreme in order to prove His intervention in answering prayer. Yet in my forty years of observing spiritual men and women who had developed roots in God, I cannot recall finding one who asked Him to indulge them ... to pamper their tastes and preferences. Wistful experimenters may theorize, but those who really know Him and mean business, ask for their needs and allow Him the privilege of "doing exceedingly, abundantly above what they ask or think."

Indeed there are those times when our Father is most extravagant in His giving. Yet the initiative is always with Him, not according to our fleshly whims or vain imaginations.

Finally, let me share this incident from our late friend, John R. Rice—prayer warrior and advocate of asking definitely. John was speaking to a crowd gathered one afteroon under the shade trees on the courthouse lawn in a Texas town. After he had earnestly tried to show that God is ready to answer our prayers when we pray definitely and expectantly, a deacon rose in the audience and said, "Brother Rice, I believe in prayer, but I do not believe God wants us to pray about literally everything. Why, you talk as if you could even pray and get a—a—(he was searching for a preposterous thing)—as if you could even get a barrel of pickels!"

The people laughed, but John went on to say plainly, "Yes, anybody who needs a barrel of pickels should pray for them, and I thank God that He has given me things a whole lot greater, and seemingly more unlikely, than a barrel of pickels."

John Rice continues to explain: "One afternoon in a Bible Conference I spoke for more than an hour on prayer and urged people to be definite, to mean business when they prayed. When the service was over, a nurse came to me . . . her face shining with a light from heaven, and said, 'So that is the way to pray, is it?'

"I answered, 'Yes, that is the way to pray!'

"Well, then, tonight I am going to have my two brothers saved!" she said. "I have been praying for them now for a year, but I have been praying, 'Lord, save my brothers before it is too late. Now I am going home and ask God to save them tonight!' And off she marched home.

He continues, "I was troubled. I thought, 'Is she risking my word, or is she really trusting God?' But she went home and spent the time in prayer, and that night had sweet assurance in her heart that God was going to save her twin brothers.

"That night an uncle came fourteen miles and was wonderfully converted. Then the nurse's mother, seeing her own brother wonderfully saved, came to the front weeping and confessed she had been a backslider. She had not been concerned about her own children as she ought to be. Then I saw coming down out of the balcony two fine young men, seventeen years old, twins. The pastor was with them and they came openly to claim Christ. It may be that God had to get the uncle—to wake up the mother, and that He needed to arouse the mother before He could reach the boys; but God did not deny the earnest, fervent prayer, the definite request, of that young nurse who asked God to save her brothers that very night, depending on the Word of God and Its clear promises."[4]

QUICKENING FROM YOUR WORD. . . read Matt.6:7-13

From this model prayer of our Lord, we see how Jesus taught His disciples to pray, using both

GENERAL REQUESTS	AND	SPECIFIC PETITIONS
THY KINGDOM COME ...		GIVE US ...
THY WILL BE DONE ...		THIS DAY ...
IN EARTH AS IN		OUR DAILY BREAD.(VS.11)
HEAVEN.(VS.10)		

How blessed to live with the long-range view, with a scope that covers heaven and earth; yet we are urged to make our very personal needs known today. This is food for meditation all day long. Hallelujah!

AWAKEN MY HEART... to ask more definitely

Father, I ask that You will enlighten every one who reads this, so that we will turn from our casual asking. I ask that we will discover what waiting on God means, so we can more clearly know what to pray for. I ask that where there is known sin or resistance to Your full will, You will even now help each one to honestly judge and turn away from whatever grieves You.

Lord, forgive us when we have had no burden or heart's desire, yet mouthed words! In so doing, we have only proved that prayer was still just a ritual—not a living fellowship with You. But we can see a change—and we are hopeful! Even as You patiently taught Your disciples how to pray definitely, so You will not leave us—until we have learned the way of asking definitely.

OVERFLOWING GRATITUDE:

Teach me to pray, Lord, Teach me to pray;
This is my heart-cry day unto day;
I long to know Thy will and Thy way;
Teach me to pray, Lord, teach me to pray.
   Living in Thee, Lord, and Thou in me,
   Constant abiding, this is my plea;
   Grant me Thy power, boundless and free,
   Power with men and power with Thee.

PRAYER REQUESTS   DATE ANSWERED

_____
_____
_____
_____
_____
_____
_____
_____
_____
_____
_____
_____
_____
_____

INSIGHTS FROM LESSON

_____
_____
_____
_____
_____
_____
_____
_____
_____
_____
_____
_____
_____
_____

DAY SIX

IF THIS JOURNAL WAS GIVEN to you by some individual or church group, you should be encouraged. It means someone is committed to praying for you each day of this journey. And you can rejoice that someone is claiming a special measure of grace for you to be totally honest with God and with yourself. Surely their praying will sustain you in those moments of weakness when you are tempted to drop out.

It is good that there is today an increasing emphasis on corporate fellowship as thousands of small "care" groups have formed. I hope this increases! Yet we must remember that our fellowship with others must not crowd out or take the place of our personal fellowship with God.

OUR LESSON TODAY moves us beyond our personal concerns, to take a brief look at those millions of God's children in other parts of the world who are not as blessed, as we, to have a Bible. It should be encouraging to realize that, even in their great lack of opportunity to read God's Word and enjoy meetings and ministry as we do, God seems to make up for their limitation through special grace.

IN OUR STORY we go behind the iron curtain into communist countries to discover how deprived, and yet how hungry many are for God's Word. More than fifty years ago when Peter Deyneka came to our home, as a young boy I was greatly moved by the boldness of this Russian emigrant. Now, I count it a joy to share this story as told by his son, Peter Deyneka, Jr.

God Satisfies
the Longing Heart

WHEN MY WIFE , Anita, and I arrived at the hotel, which happened to be the only one in the city of N (in Northern Russia)— room 205 was not ready. It was late Fall and the hotel did not look overcrowded. "Would it be possible to switch to another room that is ready?" we asked the stern clerk at the front desk.

"Nyet, nyet," she replied adamantly. "I have instructions that you are to stay in room 205. That room is being prepared for you," she insisted with a finality that left us wondering what the preparations entailed.

At this point in our travels inside the Soviet Union, we understood enough about Russia's vast system of watchers to be wary. "Don't ever say anything in your room you don't want monitored," a Christian woman who worked in a hotel had once warned. She, herself, had seen eavesdropping apparatus being installed in tourist rooms.

When we deposited our bags in room 205, Lena was sweeping the wooden floor in our room as rapidly as she could with a medieval type hand-tied twig broom that she dipped frequently in a pail of murky water.

Silver braided hair wreathed Lena's serene face. She straightened from her work and smiled when we came into the room. We spoke Russian, but she only nodded her head, turned shyly back to her work, and then quickly left the room.

The next time we saw Lena, she was standing by the hotel elevator trying to calm an angry Russian guest. "But I tell you," the Russian's face flushed furiously, "this is the second time I have been stuck in that elevator. There is no excuse for this. That elevator should be fixed!" he huffed .... the irate guest, then marched after Lena to the main desk where he repeated his complaint to the unsmiling clerk. "Tovarisch— comrad," she spoke reproachfully, "the elevator works most of the time. Why are you complaining?"

Then the next day Lena timidly stopped Anita in the hall outside room 205. "Eezvintye-forgive me," she murmured, glancing over her shoulder as she spoke. "I wanted to ask you about that little book I saw on your table . . . ."

Anita understood. Evidently we had left a booklet of the Gospel of John in Russian lying on the table beside our bed in the hotel room.

"Could you give me that little book?" Lena whispered.

"Do you want it now? Can you come with me?" Anita also kept her voice low.

Lena picked up her twig broom and slowly followed Anita down the hall as if she were coming to clean our room.

Inside Lena relaxed slightly when I switched on the radio to cover our conversation. However, she still spoke in a whisper. "I am a Lutheran. I am a verruyuscha—a believer," Lena explained, "but I have no Bible."

"Is there a Lutheran Church here in the city?" I asked.

"It was closed," Lena shrugged sadly. "I do not know of any other churches."

The night before I had visited the only Protestant church in the city of N. I quickly copied the address and handed it to Lena. Gratefully she dropped the address in her apron pocket.

"Forty years ago I came from Finland to live in Leningrad," Lena said softly. "Then I had a Bible. Thirty years ago my Bible was destroyed in World War II during the siege of Leningrad."

Lena murmured the word "seige" with terror and momentarily all the fear of those days seemed to pass across her face. "I lived through the siege," she continued, "but my Bible was destroyed." She glanced nervously at the door of our hotel room. "It is impossible to buy a Bible here in our country," she explained apologetically.

I quickly handed Lena a small Russian Bible I carried in my pocket. For a moment Lena caressed the cover with her calloused fingers. With simple sincerity she thanked us. Then she dropped the Bible in her capacious apron, lifted her broom and pail of water, and disappeared down the hall.

We didn't expect to see Lena again. But the next morning she slowly scrubbed the hall outside our room and waited for us. A beautiful smile shone from her face. "I had to see you. I must thank you again for the precious gift you gave me yesterday. For thirty years I have been praying for a Bible. I have had prayer and life is good when I pray, but now I have a Bible," she clasped her hands as if she cradled the Bible in them. "Last night I stayed up most of the night to read it." Lena could not linger any longer in the hall by room 205. She plodded down the hall with her broom and bucket of water . . . and we never saw her again."[1]

IS GOD CONCERNED FOR OTHER "LENAS"?

Millions around the world live under conditions which deprive them of having God's Word, yet they seem to find a fellowship with Him that amazes us. There is only one way to explain: God honors the heart that reaches out to know Him, even when there is a lack of His written Word.

Evangelist Terry Law after much ministry behind the iron curtain has said, "My estimate is that probably less than ten percent of the people in the underground church in the USSR have access to Scripture. Yet when the Word gets in, there seems to be a tide of the Spirit following It. There was a preacher in Siberia who preached for twelve years from the only two pages of a Bible that he had—and he saw people healed and saved."[2]

A ministry group heading into Hungary with their tiny car packed with literature, was surprised that believers—usually eager to receive all they can get—were slow to accept. Then secretly they discovered the reason: one of their number had recently been arrested for such. As they proceeded on with a bicycle they had promised to deliver to a party unknown to them, it all became clear.

God had another plan for all their literature!

To their surprise, the man they were taking the bicycle to asked if they had any extra Bibles or literature. When they showed him how much, he was beside himself with joy. He said that he belonged to a church that had no contact with the West and didn't have any access to Christian literature. The Lord had spoken to him a few months earlier that someone would be giving him a large amount of Bibles and books, and that he should begin preparing a place for them. For months he had been digging a hiding place in his cellar for what he knew would be forthcoming.[3]

While we live in such fortunate circumstances here in the West, millions behind closed doors not only survive without Bibles, but seem to enjoy God's special blessing. Another story from the People's Republic of China reveals how for eighteen long years a man named Zhang suffered in the almost unbearable conditions of labor camps. His crime? He had been arrested for starting Christian churches and house meetings. During his prison stay when he was literally cut off from the outside world, he often wondered what would happen to the believers back home. He knew that all over China the Communist government had closed church buildings, sent ministers to labor camps, and burned every Bible it found. Finally in 1978 Zhang was released from prison, and to his astonishment found that the three house meetings and three hundred believers in his county had grown to twenty house meetings and more than five thousand believers.

How shall we explain this?

Even without pastors, Bibles, church buildings or Christian literature, the Holy Spirit had directed these believers in such a way that they were able to grow, not only in numbers, but in their knowledge of the Lord.

Is it not clear, then, that in going on to know the Lord, it is not so much a lack of Bibles that hinders, as it is a lack of heart devotion to Him.

In her book, MIMOSA, Amy Carmichael tells the amazing story of a little girl in India who heard the Gospel one afternoon during a brief encounter with missionaries. In that one short hour she gave her life to this "new God", and turned from her old religion. Her father had whisked her away, lest she would hear more.

But her heart had been changed! Upon arriving home she confessed to her family that "something" strange had taken place in her. She could not explain it; how could she? She had no Bible, had no fellowship with other believers, had no instruction whatever. She only knew this "new God" had made a wonderful change within her.

What is more amazing, during the next 23 years she learned how to turn her heart toward her "new God", how to draw strength from Him even amid the most severe persecution and testings, how to survive a cruel marriage and the birth of four babies—all without the help of a Bible or Christian friends. Finally, in the over-riding providence of God she made her way back to the Dohnavur mission. Missionaries there were astounded when they discovered how God had met her continually during those long difficult years. Yes, God had proved once again that He always satisfies the longing heart.

OUR CONCLUSION: Where hungry hearts are deprived of God's Word, or limited in other ways, God seems to offer His special help to make up for the lack—because He has placed fellowship with Himself as a high priority.

CAN GOD FURNISH A TABLE?

We are again faced with this same old question which Israel faced in the wilderness. Was God able to supply food for that vast number whose exodus out of Egypt cast them utterly upon Him as their Source? We look back and marvel at God's daily provision of manna and water for them. What a table He provided for forty years. But we often forget! The same God is just as eager to provide spiritual manna today for those who look to Him. Actually, it is not so much a question of "can God furnish," as it is, "will we trust Him to provide?"

We must remember that for centuries many of God's children have not had their own Bible to "eat" from daily. Even in the early church the Epistles and Gospels, as scrolls, were available to a limited few. The Old Testament Scriptures were very scarce until Gutenberg's press in the 1500's made a wider-scale distribution possible. What about the multitudes before, who never had opportunity for personally studying God's Word?

Such questions force us to realize that millions of God's children for hundreds of years before Bibles became common property among the masses fellowshiped with God using the only "equipment" God had given to them.

What was that?

MAN IS UNIQUELY DESIGNED FOR FELLOWSHIP.

Deep within every man there is a spirit that calls out to the God who made him. The Psalmist in describing this says:

"Deep calleth unto deep . . ." (Ps.42:7).

What does he mean? It is another way of saying that something kindred calls between God and man. God's Spirit calls, and man's spirit responds and calls back as though asking for "something" to fill that inner emptiness in him. (Actually it is SOMEONE who alone can fill that inner void. We often say, man was created with a God-shaped vacuum). So, as we come to understand this call of Spirit to spirit, we can better appreciate how every man is uniquely designed for fellowship with God.

We know from certain Scriptures that man functions as body, soul and spirit. With the body he contacts the physical world about him. With the soul he contacts the realm of personality, and with his spirit he is designed to know and contact God. (1 Cor.2:10-13)

However, it is not until man is born from above, that his spirit is quickened as the Holy Spirit joins his human spirit in a union we call "the new birth." (John 3:6-8) We must all realize that, before his "new birth" mankind gropes around with a darkened, empty spirit and reaches out for "something" to fill the inner void. Only those who have been quickened in their spirit can really enjoy fellowship with God as their Father. As we have pictured, man's spirit includes the function of conscience, fellowship and intuition. In recent years there has been an increasing awareness of the important place of man's regenerated spirit in its capacity to fellowship with God.

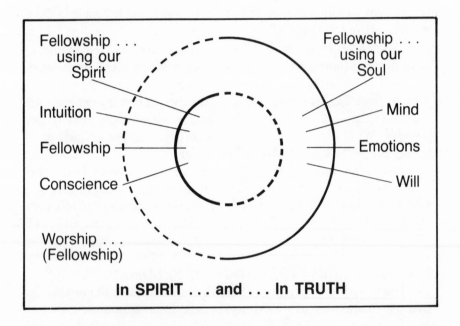

Man was also designed with a soul, which includes the function of his mind, his emotions and his will. It is important to realize that when anyone repents toward God and trusts Christ, a renewing process begins in the mind. This renewed mind can then receive renewed knowledge. (Col.3:10)

Most of us who have had the opportunity to hear and to know God's Word, appreciate the importance of truth for our minds. We almost feel it would be impossible to fellowship with God if we did not have His Word. Who could eat without bread; who would think of going to the table without food; in similar manner, God's Word has become our daily bread. It is with our renewed mind that we fellowship with God in His Word.

As we have pictured, these two distinct parts of man fulfill very important functions in his fellowship with God. The quickened spirit reaches out to know God; while the renewed mind seeks to understand more about God. Both are equally important in our fellowship with Him. This is why Jesus told the woman at the well that we must worship (fellowship with) God in spirit and in truth. (Jn.4:24)

> OUR CONCLUSION: Since God has designed man for FULLNESS OF FELLOWSHIP, it is important that he learns how, with his quickened spirit, to "touch" the Lord daily. It is of equal importance that he uses his renewed mind to feed upon the Word of God. If man emphasizes only the fellowship of the spirit and neglects the Word, he tends to become too mystical. If he emphasizes only the letter of the Word, and neglects the Spirit of Truth, he is reading without the help of His Teacher—and tends to vain rationalism.

WHAT ABOUT THOSE WHO HAVE NO BIBLE?

That God honors the hearts of those who diligently seek Him is evident! If they are limited in their knowledge of Him, as are millions behind the iron and bamboo curtains, His heart of compassion seems to reach out toward them in their limitation. God will fellowship with them in whatever light they have. Yet He will not fellowship with those who deliberately turn from light. So, to those who are more privileged to have the Word of God, such as Israel in past days, and the Church today, theirs is a much greater responsibility. How shall we escape if we neglect the Word which has been given to us?

As we read the story of Lena, and of others who long for a Bible and wait patiently for God to send one, we immediately face certain questions:

> How many days do we allow to pass without reading from His Word? Have we been careless in our fellowship with Him?

Be honest with God, as best you know how. If He has something to deal with in your life—He will uncover it, and you will know He is right and you have been wrong or careless. Confess it to

Him! And be assured that He is "faithful and just to forgive and cleanse from all unrighteousness." (1 Jn.1:9). Do it right now!

I am very concerned for those very sensitive hearts upon whom the Enemy, the accuser of the Brethren, seeks to prey and destroy openness and fellowship with God. None of us can read about Lena's longing heart and not feel compassion? In a new way we suddenly become grateful to the Lord that we have so many different versions.

That is not wrong!

Thank God that you live where the Bible is available! Remind God that you are always ready for Him to turn His searchlight upon your heart, to determine if you are wasteful, indifferent or unconcerned about the needs of others. This is what it means to "walk in the light"—so as to maintain a continuous, open fellowship with God.

Only God can help us see the true condition of our heart. Whatever He exposes of our selfishness and sin, we must be quick to confess and adjust. Please do not attempt to turn your own dim candlelight upon your heart. With the Psalmist cry out:

> Search me, O God, and know my heart: try me; and know my thoughts: And see if there be any wicked way in me, and lead me in the way everlasting. (Ps.139:23-24).

We must be more discerning. Conviction comes from the Holy Spirit's faithful ministry to us—which brings comfort when we are forgiven and cleansed. But condemnation comes from many sources. It may come from other people; it may come from the Enemy, who is the accuser of the brethren; it may come because our own weak conscience is working on inadequate knowledge.

OUR CONCLUSION: A large number of God's children live with a shadow in their fellowship, because they have not distinguished between the Holy Spirit's conviction and the Enemy's condemnation. It is not possible here to consider this important truth. If you have this shadow which might be hindering your boldness in fellowship, seek out some discerning counselor for help.

THE TESTIMONY OF ONE WHO ENJOYED FELLOWSHIP

While millions around the world have no Scriptures they can turn to daily, we have no excuse. How shall we escape, if we neglect God's Word and thereby limit our fellowship?

More than twenty years ago I read George Mueller's autobiography. This man, who is honored around the world for his unusual walk of faith, shares the method God led him to use in keeping his soul nourished every morning:

It has pleased the Lord to teach me a truth, the benefit of which I have not lost for more than fourteen years. The point is this: I saw more clearly than ever that the first great and primary business to which I ought to attend every day was to have my soul happy in the Lord. The first thing to be concerned about was not how much I might serve the Lord, or how I might glorify the Lord, but how I might get my soul into a happy state, and how my inner man might be nourished.

I saw that the most important thing I had to do was to give myself to the reading of the Word of God—not prayer, but the Word of God. And here again, not the simple reading of the Word of God so that it only passes through my mind just as water runs through a pipe, but considering what I read, pondering over it, and applying it to my heart. To meditate on it, that thus my heart might be comforted, encouraged, warned, reproved, instructed. And that thus, by means of the Word of God, whilst meditating on it, my heart be brought into experimental communion with the Lord.

I began therefore to meditate on the New Testament from the beginning early in the morning. The first thing I did, after having asked in a few words the Lord's blessing upon His precious Word, was to begin to meditate on the Word of God, searching as it were into every verse to get blessing out of it.

When we pray, we speak to God. Now, prayer, in order to be continued for any length of time in any other than a formal manner, requires, generally speaking, a measure of strength or godly desire; and the season, therefore, when this exercise of the soul can be most effectively performed is after the inner man has been nourished by meditation on the Word of God, where we find our Father speaking to us, to encourage us, to comfort us, to instruct us, to humble us, to reprove us.

By the blessing of God, I ascribe to this mode the help and strength which I have had from God to pass in peace through deeper trials, in various ways, than I had ever had before.

How different, when the soul is refreshed and made happy early in the morning, from what it is when, without spiritual preparation, the service, the trials, and the temptations of the day come upon me! (written May 9th, 1841)

The Psalmist pleads:
> "O send out thy *light* and thy *truth;*
>   let them lead me;
> let them bring me into thy holy hill,
>   and to thy tabernacles.
> Then will I go unto the altar of God,
>   unto God my exceeding joy;
> yea, upon the harp will I praise thee,
>   O God my God."

We ponder!

Why does he speak of both light and truth? What is the difference? Perhaps it is light for our spirit and truth for our mind. These two will lead us into joyous communion at His altar!

We must remember that it is impossible for man to enter into fellowhip with God until his spirit has been enlightened in the work of regeneration.

"For thou wilt light my candle: the Lord my God will enlighten my darkness" (Ps.18:28).

". . . in Thy light shall we see light . . ." (Ps.36:9).

"If we walk in the light as He is
   in the light we have fellowship . . ."(1 Jn.1:7).

AWAKEN MY HEART .... to the need for both truth and light.

Father, I have so often limited You by my narrowness. Now I can see how You will nurture any one who longs for fellowship, even under the most limiting circumstances—as Lena and Mimosa faced. You are my God, utterly worthy of my trust. It gives me such rest to realize that You are bigger than all our explanations of You. I begin to see that truth for my mind and light for my spirit should always work as a team. I see how truth received without light becomes lifeless doctrine; but with divine light it becomes revelation. Thank You for both—they shall lead me.

OVERFLOWING GRATITUDE

Praise the Saviour, ye who know Him;
Who can tell how much we owe Him?
Gladly let us render to Him
    All we have and are.

Jesus is the name that charms us;
He for conflicts fits and arms us;
Nothing moves and nothing harms us;
    When we trust in Him.

Trust in Him, ye saints for ever;
He is faithful, changing never;
Neither force nor guile can sever
    Those He loves from Him.

Keep us, Lord, oh keep us cleaving
To Thyself, and still believing,
Till the hour of our receiving
    Promised joys in heaven.

Then we shall be where we would be;
Then we shall be what we should be;
Things which are not now, nor could be,
    Then shall be our own.
                (T. Kelly)

PRAYER REQUESTS   DATE ANSWERED

_____
_____
_____
_____
_____
_____
_____
_____
_____
_____
_____
_____
_____
_____

DAY SEVEN

WE ARE LEARNING that our fellowship with God is not just for enjoyment, but it is also the way in which God prepares us for our life work. It is His schoolroom where we discover and joyfully accept His ways, where we learn to depend upon Him as our only source, and where we learn the importance of maintaining a hidden life before Him.

IN OUR LESSON TODAY . . . we see there is both a general and a very special training. If we are only yielded to God for a general work, we will get run-of-the-mill training, but if we want to be specially used by Him, God has some very unique training, as we shall see in the life of His servant, Joe Evans.

Dr. V. Raymond Edman, the late president of Wheaton College, explains how his close friend, Joe Evans, was prepared for a very special intercessory ministry.

Joyfully Accepting All God's Ways

THE SHOE LACE had broken again! Young Joe Evans, the Welshman, viewed the portion of the lace that was in his hand and that which remained in his shoe. He prayed quietly, "Dear Lord, Thou knowest that I need a new pair of shoe laces."

That was all, and it was most certainly true. The laces had broken before and had been knotted to extend their span of usefulness. Now it was difficult to knot them again and make them serviceable.

Did the owner of the shoes not have enough money to buy a pair of shoelaces? The answer is, "No." In utter faithfulness to his Lord, whom he had received as Savior in the Welsh revival of 1904, Joe had given up secular employment and had come from his homeland to the United States. He was firmly persuaded that God had called him into His service. Therefore he had entered Bible school in order to prepare. Now he had begun a ministry as Bible teacher and evangelist in the city of Boston.

Those were days of deep testing for the Lord's servant. He learned very early the meaning of Paul's testimony:

"I know how to be abased and live humbly in straitened circumstances, and I know also how to enjoy plenty and live in abundance. I have learned in any and all circumstances the secret of facing every situation, whether well-fed or going hungry, having a sufficiency and to spare or going without and being in want" (Phil.4:12 A.N.T.).

71

Joe was learning what it meant to be physically hungry that he might trust implicitly the One who long ago had fed five thousand men plus women and children with five loaves and two little fishes. Joe suffered need that he might know the Faithful One who had promised, "My God shall supply all your need according to His riches in glory by Christ Jesus" (Phil.4:19).

Should one pray for a matter as small as a pair of shoelaces? I think so, for the principle of faith is not concerned with quantity, but rather with quality. The Lord Jesus taught that if we have faith as a grain of mustard seed, then great things can happen. The Savior was not emphasizing the minute size of the seed, but rather its vitality. It was a living substance and represented a living faith. If He had desired only to stress the matter of minuteness, He would have likened faith to a grain of sand.

On the part of young Joe Evans there was no repetition of the request for shoelaces. He went about the Lord's work with the shoes and laces as they were, content to make known his request to only the Most High.

A week went by, and then came a letter from a friend in California. Its contents were two-fold—a faltering apology for writing a letter under a strong sense of compulsion, and a pair of shoelaces. "Somehow or other, I cannot get away from the impression that I should include these shoelaces in my letter, and yet what a ridiculous thing for me to do," declared the writer.

Ridiculous? Not in the least, for the Holy Spirit, in faithfulness to the petition of His servant in Boston, had found someone clear across the continent who could hear the request and be humble enough to obey implicitly.

It was through lessons of this kind that Joe Evans learned both to pray and to trust. Over the years he had said to us again and again, "There is no use of praying unless we trust. To pray is to ask, to make known our petition to the Lord. Then our part is to trust that He has heard and will answer in His own time and way. We must pray and trust!"

Another incident from Joe's life: On one occasion during those first years in America, Joe went from Boston to visit with some elderly friends in the Adirondacks and to have a brief holiday. The place served its purpose well for rest and for study of the Word. The detachment from the outside world was quite complete. There were no radios, and newspapers were very slow in arriving at the home.

One morning as the Lord's servant arose, he was aware of a great burden of prayer on his heart. He excused himself and went out in the woods to pray. The burden of prayer increased throughout the day rather than diminishing or disappearing. At first there was prayer for many causes: the Lord's work at Boston, fellow servants at home and abroad, missionaries on far-flung fields of earth, those in physical and spiritual need, and those in financial necessity.

However, as hours went on, and the burden of prayer increased, he began to concentrate his intercession on behalf of His Majesty, King Edward VII. With great agony of soul, he prayed earnestly for the salvation of the King until there came the release of full assurance that prayer had been answered. All alone in those lovely mountains in New York, he was persuaded that God had heard and answered prayer on behalf of His Majesty.

The following day, word came from a Welsh companion. "King Edward is dead!"

"I did not know the king was ill," replied the surprised Joe Evans. Then he related to his friend what had transpired in the previous two days. His friend expressed scepticism on the matter, since the actions of the King and his attitude toward the Gospel rendered doubtful any interest in the salvation of his soul.

Many years later Dr. Joe Evans and I (Pres. Edman continues) were having dinner with the late Dr. J. Gregory Mantle of England. In the course of our conversation, Dr. Mantle, who had never heard this incident by Dr. Evans, inquired, "Joe, did you know that King Edward VII was saved on his deathbed?"

"Tell me about it," was the reply.

"The King was in France when he was taken ill. He was brought to England, and there was hope that he might recover. However, a turn came for the worse. At that time, His Majesty called one of his lords-in-waiting and ordered him to go to Paternoster Row and secure for him a copy of a tract which his mother, Queen Victoria, had given to him when he was a lad. It was entitled, "A Sinners Friend." After much searching, the lord-in-waiting found the tract, brought it to His Majesty, and found upon reading it, King Edward made earnest repentance and received the Lord Jesus as his Saviour."

Thereupon Dr. Evans told his part of that story.

Is it astonishing that the Spirit of God would have to seek far afield to find some intercessor on behalf of the King so that the many prayers offered by his mother should be answered?[1]

WHAT A DAY IT WILL BE when heaven's curtain is finally pulled back, and we can see all those hidden ones who have faithfully labored in prayer. Indeed, we shall be surprised as we behold many, like Joe Evans, who have patiently accepted God's preparation that they might be available for life's emergencies: such as "standing in the gap"—interceding for those in desperate need.

God's ways are so different from ours! The world says, prove that you are being used by God. Be successful! God says, prove that you can be faithful to me—even in little things. It is a question we must all face. Am I wholly content to leave my "success" in God's hands? I am convinced that in this matter of accepting God's ways, nothing hinders us so much as the lust to be successful—now.

Writing in his day to the Corinthian church, Paul exhorted, ". . . it is required in stewards that a man be found FAITHFUL . . . ." What would he write about many today, who have blatantly and boldly substituted their own version, ". . . that a man be found SUCCESSFUL."

I wonder!

THE CRITICAL ISSUE IS OUR WRONG SEEKING. When we seek the applause of men, we cannot please God. If we seek to be a success in the eyes of the world, we shall come short of that divine fruitfulness God intends for us.

In fulfilling our own calling each of us will give account to God—the only One who can read the motives of our heart. We can be sure, if we make faithfulness to Him as our goal, God will take care of whatever fulfillment we need.

We must remember that success is not wrong; seeking it is!

God forbid that we should ever exalt failure or excuse our weaknesses under the cloak of being "more spiritual". Surely the great snare today is our confusing. . .

THE PROPER GOAL. . . . (with) . . . . THE BY-PRODUCT	
Seek ye first the kingdom of God	. . . . and all these things shall be added (Matt.6:33)
If ye be willing and obedient	. . . . ye shall eat the good of the land (Isa.1:19)
In ALL thy ways acknowledge Him	. . . . and He shall direct thy paths (Prov.3:6)
Thou shalt meditate day and night that thou mayest observe to do. . . .	. . . . then, thou shalt make thy way prosperous . . . and have good success (Jos.1:8)
His delight is in the law, and he meditates therein day and night	. . . . and he shall be like a tree, shall be fruitful . . . and prosper (Ps.1:3)
Therefore being justified by faith	. . . . . we have peace with God through Jesus (Rom.5:1)

How easy it is to fall into the snare of wrong seeking. Perhaps unwittingly we emphasize the by-product, when we should be seeking the proper goals. Go over the list of by-products again. How often do we seek for the things He promises will be "added"; how often do we seek to "eat the good of the land" but ignore willingness and obedience; we seek direction, prosperity, success and peace, yet they are promised only to those who seek God first.

Remember, we are not saying that any of these by-products are wrong, they are just dangerous for us—if we have not fulfilled the divine requirement first. Did you notice we are "to acknowledge Him in ALL our ways" not just those that are convenient?

Let us consider these words from a man who surely understood proper seeking and its rewards. Though his life ended early and he was scarcely appreciated in his time, today his writings have come into prominence. Oswald Chambers exposes the shallowness of our day:

> "Jesus Christ says in effect, don't rejoice in successful service, but rejoice because you are rightly related to Me. The snare in Christian work is to rejoice in successful service... Keep your relationship right with Him, then whatever circumstances you are in, and whoever you meet day by day, He is pouring rivers of living water through you and it is of His mercy that He does not let you know it."

> "The great enemy to the Lord Jesus Christ in the present day is this conception of practical work that has not come from the New Testament, but from the systems of the world in which endless energy and activities are insisted upon, but no private life with God. It is bred into us that we have to do exceptional things for God, but we have not. We have to be exceptional in the ordinary things, to be holy in mean streets among mean people."

NOW LET US SUMMARIZE SOME OF GOD'S WAYS.

(1) As we learn to trust God, even in little things that may seem foolish, He prepares us for greater responsibility.

(2) As we allow God to develop our hidden life before Him, we become available to be used any time and in any way. We can rest assured that He will!

(3) As we accept God's yardstick for measuring "success", He will give us inner quietness and contentment—even when we are hidden and unknown, and our friends bask in the limelight.

(4) As we seek first His kingdom, we can expect the by-products to be added. Thus we reject the snare of wrong seeking.

(5) As we accept new each lesson—whether painful or blessed—we shall begin to realize how each was uniquely designed for a special purpose. It will then not seem strange that those who insist upon taking an easier way will merely get a *general* training, while those— like the apostle Paul— who insist on living for God's fullness, will be prepared by some *unusual* training for their special calling.

QUICKENING FROM YOUR WORD: Read 1 Cor.4:2-7 L.B.

Perhaps we can better understand the heart-cry of Paul when he writes: "Now the most important thing about a servant is that he does just what his master tells him to do. What about me? Have I been a good servant? Well, I don't worry over what you think about this, or what anyone else thinks. I don't even trust my own judgment on this point. My conscience is clear, but even that isn't the final proof. It is the Lord Himself who must examine me and decide.

"So be careful not to jump to conclusions before the Lord returns as to whether someone is a good servant or not. When the Lord comes, He will turn on the light so that everyone sees exactly what each one of us is really like, deep down in our hearts. Then everyone will know why we have been doing the Lord's work. At that time God will give to each one whatever praise is coming to him." (1 Cor.4:2-7 L.B.)

Do you ever copy things into the vacant spots in your Bible? More than twenty years ago I added this portion from a devotional book by Watchman Nee. It fit into the empty place at the end of the book of Hosea:

". . . he shall grow up as a lily, and
cast forth his roots as Lebanon" (Hos.14:5).

"Here united in the child of God are two contrasting characters. Above ground, as it were, is the simple unsophisticated life of trust and faith represented by the lily of God's planting. That is what men see. Yet buried deep down out of sight, giving to this frail plant a wholly unsuspected strength, are the massive roots of the cedars. Here surely is the paradox of a life in which the Cross is known. Outwardly it is fragile as the lily blooming on the earth—but secretly there is a hundred times more below ground.

"This is the test. How much of my life is seen? When men look on the surface, have they seen the whole or is there something more? Have I in the unseen a secret history with God? Men take account only of the lily blooming in its weakness. God is concerned with the roots, that they may be cedar-like in strength."[2]

Indeed, there is a difference between what the world sees and measures by its own yardstick, and what God sees as fruitfulness from His viewpoint.

FATHER, AWAKEN MY HEART to accept all Your ways— even those that seem so contrary to my desires. Even when friends are achieivng apparent success, I want to keep my eyes upon You and wait for that day when all things will be measured according to eternal values.

Forgive me . . . when I have complained about the inexplainable lessons You have sent for my inner preparation. In observing the hidden life of Joe Evans, I am convinced that You are waiting— eager to use everyone who is available and prepared. In observing Joe Evans, I am much encouraged by the manner in which he touched many issues in prayer until he finally came to center in on the need of King Edward VII. Only then did he sense that he had touched the real issue in prayer.

My request! Lord, will You develop that kind of sensitivity in my spirit, even as my mind is searching about for Your burden.

Yes, my heart begins to rejoice when I realize that You have invited man into a glorious partnership through intercession. I do not want to appear as an elitist in the eyes of others who do not understand, yet I will accept this hidden life before You; I can fully trust You that mine will not be a wasted life. Eternity will reveal all things!

OVERFLOWING GRATITUDE

In the secret of His presence,
   How my soul delights to hide!
Oh, how precious are the lessons
   Which I learn at Jesus' side!
Earthly cares can never vex me,
   Neither trials lay me low;
For when Satan comes to tempt me,
   To the secret place I go,
   To the secret place I go.

When my soul is faint and thirsty,
    'Neath the shadow of His wing.
There is cool and pleasant shelter,
    And a fresh and crystal spring;
And my Savior rests beside me,
    As we hold communion sweet;
If I tried, I could not utter
    What He says when thus we meet
    What He says when thus we meet.

Would you like to know the sweetness
    Of the secret of the Lord?
Go and hide beneath His shadow:
    This shall then be your reward;
And when-e'er you leave the silence
    Of that happy meeting place,
You must mind and bear the image
    Of the Master in your face,
    Of the Master in your face.
            (George C. Stebbins)

PRAYER REQUESTS   DATE ANSWERED

_____

_____

_____

_____

_____

_____

_____

_____

_____

_____

_____

_____

_____

_____

_____

_____

_____

_____

INSIGHTS FROM LESSON

_____

_____

_____

_____

_____

_____

_____

_____

_____

_____

_____

_____

_____

_____

_____

_____

_____

_____

_____

_____

DAY EIGHT

EACH DAY WE UNCOVER another facet of God's character. We continue to appreciate why knowing who God chiefly is, is so necessary if we are to participate with Him in His purposes and His ways. In knowing who He is, we come to understand the two sides of His nature: His love and His wrath; His compassion and His warning.

DOES GOD ALWAYS WARN before He sends judgment? To truly know Him as Father is to understand His compassion and mercy. His very character requires that He warn those He loves. We must see how He sometimes goes to great lengths to get the attention of those who are dull and insensitive. Surely He is doing this today!

DOES GOD ALWAYS SEND JUDGMENT on those who reject His warning? To be consistent with His character He must. Because of our dullness we may not always recognize His warnings, yet we can be sure that God is righteous as well as merciful. This explains why He reacts so quickly toward those who mock the sacrifice of His Son.

TO DEVELOP AN EAR TO HEAR when He is warning is surely the urgent need among God's people today. Those who obediently walk in His ways, will develop an ear to hear what the Spirit is now saying unto the Church.

IN THIS STORY, Dr. Edman explains how his personal friends, the Hartmans, were spared because of a sensitive ear.

More Attentive in Hearing

IT WAS EASTER SEASON, 1902. Martinique is a French island in the Caribbean Sea, a few islands south of Puerto Rico. With a beautiful large bay where the waters are almost perfect, and the tropical vegetation creates a paradise, it had become the playground for the rich of Europe who often came to spend their holidays in revelry.

This season found twelve big ships from Europe docked in its bay, while the passengers were on shore celebrating Lent season with all the wickedness that often accompanies Mardi Gras.

Because God was not willing that any should perish, He sent two young men from Canada. When their boat arrived in Martinique, the immigration officer asked them what they intended to do while in Martinique. "Preach God's Word," they answered.

But such preaching the islanders did not want, because it would interfere with their revellings and make them uncomfortable in their sins. The officer told them, "You will not soil our land by even stepping on it. You stay on your boat, and when it pulls out of harbor, you pull out with it."

Meanwhile, on land the people were given to drunkenness and gross immorality, with open scoffing and blasphemy against anything religious. It was discovered later that a sow had been sacrificed on Good Friday in the cathedral as a burlesque of the crucifixion of Jesus.

This was more than God would take! Almost immediately the tall mountain, Pelee, overlooking the bay, started to smoke, as though a volcano was going to erupt. It had been inactive during

historic times except for two minor eruptions in 1762 and 1851. Now the people were frightened and sent scientists up to investigate the possibility of an eruption. They were unanimous, "It was cool as ever—there was no danger." They returned saying, "Go on in your dancing and pleasures, everything is safe." Once again the music and revelry broke loose in full swing.

Three days later the Canadian boat pulled out of harbor with the two evangelists on board. They had just passed the three mile limit when GOD ANSWERED IN JUDGMENT. The whole side of that huge mountain blew out and in 60 seconds time covered the entire city like a fog with glowing, incandescent particles. So extraordinary was the intensity of the electrical manifestations associated with the violence of the blast that magnetic disturbances were transmitted as far as the North and South Pole within two minutes.

Only two people survived the catasrophe which wiped out the entire capital city. Those were prisoners in solitary confinement, held in the deepest dungeon of the city jail. One of these was a preacher who was discovered when they cleared away the rocks and debris.

Fire from the volcano fell on islands 125 miles away where the natives had to stand in their fields and beat out the fires set by flying cinders that fell. The boat carrying the two young men was burning from stem to stern when it reached the next island of St. Lucia. What a solemn warning to our generation that God will not stand mocking the sacrifice of His Son, Jesus![1]

BUT THERE IS MORE TO THIS STORY not recorded in usual accounts. For months I had attempted to search out other aspects of this incident. Surely God must have some further lessons to teach from this tragedy. Then, as by sovereign direction, I found a book in my father's library, written by Dr. Edman of Wheaton College. It gives this personal testimony of how John H. Hartman narrowly escaped destruction when Mt. Pelee blew her top.

He writes: At the turn of the century, the Hartmans were missionaries in the West Indies. Several times a year Mr. Hartman traveled by the small inter-island steamer to visit congregations of believers, since he was a settled pastor at his home station, but also an itinerant missionary to many a congregation throughout the islands in the Caribbean.

"Only once," he said to me, "did Mrs. Hartman ever ask me not to go on one of those trips. Many a time she was ill with tropical fever, to be sure; but only on one occasion did she beg me not to go as I had planned."

"I explained to her that I had no alternative but to go. The steamer went only once a month. The previous month I had sent letters to each congregation along the way to inform them that on the next trip I would come for some services.

"The steamer remained in a given harbor for a day or two, sometimes more. Each local congregation knew approximately the day of arrival and would send word to those scattered in towns, villages and plantations. In those days we had no wireless or radio service, and no air mail. Either I had to go, or else disappoint every congregation throughout the islands.

He went on to explain how Mrs. Hartman was willing for him to go if he insisted. However, she expressed great apprehension for him. Though she was a very cheerful and optimistic person, she had grave apprehension that he would never return should he go on that trip.

"Finally," he went on to say, "reluctantly I agreed to stay in Barbados. I watched the little steamer sail from the harbor, and my heart went out to the many Christians who would be disappointed in not meeting me as it arrived on one island and another.

"In the meantime, entirely unknown to me, much had been taking place on the island of Martinique . . . with mounting wickedness and depravity, there came increasingly violent persecution of the believers, subjecting them to physical harm and imprisonment as well as insolence and insults from their fellow citizens. The persecution grew so intense that the Christians had felt they could no longer remain in the city.

"As a result they gathered together what few belongings they could take with them and went as a group to St. Pierre. They obeyed literally the Scripture, 'When they persecute you in this city, flee ye into another.' (Matt.10:23)

"I wonder," said Mr. Hartman thoughtfully, " if they gave much thought to the verse which follows the injunction of shaking off the dust of their feet. Matthew 10:15 declares, 'Verily I say unto you, It shall be more tolerable for the land of Sodom and Gomorrah in the day of judgment than for that city.'

"Their principal concern was for me. They knew that I would be arriving in a few days on the boat, and they had no way of telling me where they had gone or why. They did their best by leaving a message with some to be delivered to me on board ship, if indeed their neighbors would take the trouble so to do. They then went on foot to another part of the island. Some days after arriving at their destination, they witnessed from afar the tremendous and terrifying explosion of Mt. Pelee."

The little congregation of Christians was overwhelmed with sorrow, for they believed that their pastor had perished in the destruction. They learned that every ship in the harbor had been destroyed, that the inter-island steamer in particular had burned at the wharf, and that there were no survivors. It was not until two months later that their sorrow turned into joy when they welcomed their pastor and learned from him the wonderful story of God's deliverance because of divine guidance given to Mrs. Hartman.

Thank God! They and their pastor had been saved from the sudden destruction that annihilated their city and its inhabitants.[2]

WHAT A CLEAR MESSAGE TO US! Some were delivered, but others were destroyed. It was as though God extended two hands—the Hand of grace and the Hand of judgment. Some would choose God's way and receive life; others chose their own way and received the consequences—judgment.

We might ask, did God perform a special favor for Christians on that island, or does He always work like this? There are some important issues we need to consider.

DOES GOD ALWAYS SEND WARNING? Yes, because of His character, compassion, and consistency, He sends warning before He sends judgment. We need only look at the many incidents in His Word which demonstrate that He keeps all promises: those of promised blessing, and those of promised judgment. It seems the more we know Him as our Father, the more we can appreciate how deliberately He fulfills these verses:

> Surely the Lord will do nothing, but He revealeth His secrets unto His servants the prophets. Amos 3:7
> Shall I hide from Abraham that thing which I am to do? Gen.18:17
> Wherefore I will plead with you and with your children's children. Jer.2:1
> Whoso harkeneth unto Me shall dwell securely and shall be quiet without fear and evil. Prov.1:33
> Jehovah was very angry with Solomon . . . for he was no longer interested in the Lord God . . . who had appeared to him twice to warn him specifically against worshiping other gods. But he hadn't listened . . ." 1 Kings 11:9 L.B.

Indeed we search to find even one instance in God's Word when He did not go to some length to warn before He intervened in judgment.

WE MUST BE CAREFUL, for we are prone to emphasize one side of truth and neglect the other. While it is important to develop confidence in God's character, that He will always warn, it is dangerous to remain preoccupied with only this. It is equally important for us to develop a listening ear to hear. On the one side is God's faithfulness, on the other side is our accountability. How often we have loved to prove one side of His character, yet neglected the other side. The same Father who is merciful to warn, is also righteous to judge those who continue to spurn His Word and His ways. All Scripture teaches us that God is ...

compassionate,	but also	demanding
merciful,	but also	full of wrath
loving,	but also	jealous
faithful,	but also	righteous.

It is evident that we usually hear the side of truth that is pleasant and most convenient. Our ears are not tuned to anything else. If hearing God's voice seems to be our problem today, consider how He has (most) always had this same problem with His people!

In the days of Jeremiah, God warned Israel continuously for thirty years that captivity was coming. It finally got to the place that whenever they met him they mockingly asked, "Well, Jeremiah, what is the sad news from the Lord today?" Jer.23:32 L.B.

Is it not true, the more we know our own hearts, the more we can realize how irritating it was for Israel to constantly be reminded of their folly. No wonder they mocked him! No wonder he was known as the weeping prophet! He was as a kill-joy—like a constant pricking-pricking in their side!

Like many "moderns" they wanted to hear only the positive message that God is always faithful to His people and to His promise that, "We shall dwell securely and shall be quiet without fear or evil ...."

Yet that was only half of the message; there was also this condition: "Whoso harkeneth unto Me ...." During those long years of enjoying God's blessing, Israel had become complacent. Were they not the chosen people of God, the apple of His eye, the one He had always favored with blessing! How they revelled in God's faithfulness and His promises! But they had become blinded—most insensitive and indifferent to their own accountability to Him.

In the days of Moses, God launched their wilderness pilgrimage by giving them this simple instruction: "If thou wilt diligently hearken unto the voice of the Lord..." which translated more exactly means, "...if listening thou wilt listen" Exod.15:26. We remember their sad history; for forty years they wandered in the barren wilderness. Hearts that could have learned to rejoice in their testing were instead hardened. What an opportunity to know Him more intimately and to know His ways! Like so many of us, they refused to listen!

In the days of Noah, while he built the ark and preached righteousness for one hundred years, God was speaking to that generation. They would not hear! Even that very last week before the flood, they had a seven-day advance warning, yet to no avail.

In the days of Abraham, when God came down to visit and announced His intentions of destroying Sodom, we recall that only Lot and his family responded to the warning and fled from the city. Yet even Lot's wife did not heed God's warning to not look back when leaving the city. She looked back, and became a pillar of salt on the plains—a reminder to all—of God's sure judgment when we fail to heed all that He has said.

In the days of Jonah, we have one of those rare occurences of a people who heard God speak. After Jonah recovered from his own wayward escapade, and finally preached his warning to Nineveh, there was an amazing repentance from the king down to all his people. What an encouraging reminder for us—God's longsuffering is sure when man hears and repents. Nineveh did!

In the days of Amos, God warned that He would not forever hide His face from wickedness, but "will cause you to go into captivity." Amos even described their pitiful condition: "Behold, the days come ... that I will send a famine in the land, not a famine of bread, nor a thirst for water, but of HEARING the Word of the Lord" Amos 8:11.

For years I pondered what Amos could have meant when he spoke of a famine of hearing. Now I realize how very much we are like the people of his generation. In his day scribes were most diligent in preparing the Scriptures for God's people. Israel rejoiced in knowing they were a people more privileged than all the nations of the earth, for they possessed the Oracles of God (His Word). Indeed, they did have His Word—both written and prophetic—but they were guilty of not *hearing* God's voice in that Word.

How much we are like them! By the media of T V and radio, the abundance of Bibles and books, the increase of meetings, it would seem there is no famine of God's Word. However this abundance only focuses our attention to God's real warning: there is a famine—not of the Word—but of hearing!

SOMETIMES JUDGMENT IS VERY SUDDEN—WHY?

God's judgment upon the wickedness of Martinique was most severe and sudden. With other wicked nations it seems the cup of iniquity filled slowly. Why? Was there some difference?

First, God is very jealous about the loving sacrifice of His Son on the Cross. The same God who was merciful in freely giving us such love, is also quick to judge those who mock or spurn the sacrifice of His blood. Imagine! What blatant mockery to sacrifice a hog on that "holy" day! It was more than God could bear, and He sent sudden destruction when Mt. Pelee blew her top. Such mockery has been suddenly met with judgment on other occasions throughout the course of history.

Second, it seems that God deals in severity and suddeness, when His governmental authority is openly challenged. In Numbers 16, Korah and two hundred leaders of the congregation assembled themselves against Moses. They railed on him with an uncontrollable flood of unrestrained words. In this we see two different degrees of rebellion: though Miriam spoke against Moses, her words were restrained; and though she was disgraced, she could be restored. But it was different for Korah and his cohorts: "the earth opened her mouth and (suddenly) swallowed them up . . . " Num.16:32.

Third, it seems that God deals most severely with any sexual perversion that destroys the family. Why? Because His paternal purpose governs all! Adam was a father; Noah was a father; Abraham was a father. Whatever rejects or challenges fatherhood and the development of a family, is an open challenge to God's Fatherhood and His eternal purpose for a family.

It is obvious that homosexuality as an alternate lifestyle, openly defies God's intention for the increase of His family. Sodom was suddenly destroyed because of sexual sins! If God does not deal with this present disgrace of abortion, He will have to apologize to Sodom. Could it be that A.I.D.S. is just the beginning of that judgment? *Oh God, let it be averted—but if not, let nothing hinder the fulfillment of Your eternal purpose. Would You open our ears to be more attentive in hearing what You are saying to Your church today.*

THREE HINDRANCES TO OUR HEARING

First, there is a pre-occupaton with doing our own thing. Everyone has his own project for the Lord, and beckons the help of others. These words from a medical doctor illustrate just how unconsciously we are centered in doing our own thing. After attending his own pastor for six months, the doctor felt led to say to him, "Pastor, you've been a very busy man. It may be that God has had something to say to you, but you were too busy to listen, so He has had to lay you on your back, that you might hear His voice."

As the doctor was leaving the house, these same words suddenly struck him! He himself was a busy man—far too busy—and did not give much time to listening for the voice of God. Immediately he determined to practice what he had preached to his pastor. "And from that day," he said, "I have sat at the close of each day for an hour in the quiet of my study. Not to speak to God, but to listen to what He might say to me, and to lay the whole day's work open to His gaze." How many are too busy doing their own thing—to even heed their own advice.

Like the woodsman who was too busy to sharpen his axe, we are too busy working for God to listen to what He wants done. We seek to siphon off any satisfaction we can get from our work, instead of finding our satisfaction in pleasing Him.

Second, we unconsciously develop "selective hearing," which means that we hear what we like and tune out the rest. How aptly a lady exposed her problem: "When I seek to get quiet before God ... I hear things I don't want to hear. I guess that explains why I do all the talking." While that may not describe us, are we not adept in hearing about God's great faithfulness in fulfilling His promises, yet so dull in hearing about our responsibility to Him and His Word.

Jonah had this problem of "selective hearing." When God announced that He was sending him to warn Nineveh, as a devout Jew he had no room in his heart for meeting the need of a wicked Gentile city. Only after his miraculous episode in the belly of the fish is he willing to listen. God's directions had not changed: Arise, and go! The first time he had half-obeyed. He arose—and fled!

Third, ours must be a continuous hearing, not a once-for-all-receiving. Most of us are prone to assume that once we have received a word from God, that is enough. We are like the little boy who was being punished, "But I did listen, Daddy, I didn't know you were going to speak again." He had heard what he wanted, and then run off.

QUICKENING FROM YOUR WORD: God is not wasting words when He says: "Today if you will hear his voice ...." It is His way of warning us to listen again and again—everyday. Likewise Isaiah reminds us, "The Lord awakens me morning by morning, He awakens my ear to listen as a disciple"(50:4). It is one thing to take a step, but walking implies continuous action. "Your ears will hear a word behind you, This is the way, walk ye in it . . ." (30:21). Thus it is in walking with Him daily, we learn to hear His voice. And if we expect to hear more, we must first walk out what we have already heard.

I am alarmed! Many in this hour, even among God's choice servants, have heard God speak in the past; but they have not had a fresh word for a long time. We need to be concerned when hearing is not continuous. When messages sound like an experience from the past, we need to be alarmed. Above all we need to be tuned in to what God is saying NOW, as His present truth for this hour.

AWAKEN MINE—TO BE A HEARING HEART

Father, I do acknowledge that few like the voice of a prophet. I do not! Yet, I recognize when I hear one who speaks for You. I realize he is sent to awaken those who are asleep in Zion, and I have often been at ease. His voice has no pleasing tone—it stirs and aggravates. Yet, I know (inwardly) when truth is spoken. I choose to hear, even though I often feel sure it could have been said with more tact—with more love. I know we must all be driven from our hiding places, from our indifference. Forgive me when my ears have been full of wax, dull and so insensitive to Your pleadings.

Lord, when I consider Your faithfulness in delivering Your children from Martinique, I can rejoice; but when I consider Your righteous judgment on those who mocked the sacrifice of Your Son, I am caused to worship You in Your ways. What value You place on Your supreme Sacrifice at Calvary!

Do I hear You saying that You need more watchmen who will warn others of the dangerous hours ahead? You also want those who will intercede for the central purpose of Your heart; who will not become confused with good things that need to be done, but will give priority to that primary thing You have called them to. And Lord, I ask that not only my own ears be opened, but that You will also open the ears of others to hear and obey. If indeed a famine of hearing Your Word is our present problem, I stand with You in meeting this need.

OVERFLOWING GRATITUDE fills my heart, and I join with the poet who pleads:

> Open my ears, that I may hear
> Voices of truth Thou sendest clear;
> And while the wave-notes fall on my ear,
> Everything false will disappear.
> Silently now I wait for Thee,
> Ready, my God, Thy will to see;
> Open my ears, illumine me, Spirit Divine!
> (Clara H. Scott)

> 'Waken my heart, that I may see,
> All that Your Word has promised me;
> Then let me also understand,
> How to fulfill all You have planned.
> Silently now I wait for Thee,
> Ready, my God, Thy plan to see;
> 'Waken my heart, illumine me, Spirit Divine!
> (author)
> (Open your hymnal and sing the rest)

PRAYER REQUESTS   DATE ANSWERED

_____
_____
_____
_____
_____
_____
_____
_____
_____
_____
_____
_____
_____
_____
_____
_____
_____
_____
_____

DAY NINE

WHEN FELLOWSHIP IS REAL, it will mean we are allowing our whole life to be open before Him—as a book. We can expect that God will awaken us to see how we are living short of eternal values; how we are slaves of self-centered goals, how often we even become slaves of a "religious busyness" that produces barrenness, while all the time confessing we are under the Lordship of Jesus Christ.

IN OUR LESSON we consider why so many of God's children are trapped in spiritual passivity, why so many who enjoy much spiritual knowledge do not live in the good of what they know. Something is wrong!

The critical issue is our willingness to obey God in every area, not just selective areas we may choose.

TODAY . . . we meet Corrie Ten Boom, beloved by millions around the world for her straight-forwardness and utter simplicity. Now her last prayer has been answered, and she has entered into the presence of the One she loved and obeyed so implicitly. We feel sure she finished her race triumphantly, having proved His faithfulness to the end. These selected incidents from her journey illustrate how we too can expect God's supply when we meet ONE PRIOR CONDITION.

One Prior Condition

ON MY TRIP to the Far East, I was in Formosa. The Lord told me very clearly that I had to work in several countries and that I should buy an air ticket. But I had no money! Since the Lord is my Shepherd, He is also my Treasurer, and He is very wealthy.

Sometimes He tries my faith, but when I am obedient, then the money comes just in time. "The cattle upon a thousand hills" belong to Him. Sometimes, when I need money, I just say, "Father, I believe that You must sell from the cattle on one of Your mountains," and then He answers my prayer.

At the travel agency I said to the girl at the desk: "Will you write down the names of these places for which I need an air ticket? First to Hong Kong, then to Sydney in Australia, then to Cape Town in South Africa, Tel Aviv in Israel and Auckland in New Zealand, then Amsterdam in Holland.

She wrote it down and then asked: "What is your end destination?"

"Heaven," I answered.

"How do you write that?" she asked.

I spelled H E A V E N. When she had written it down, she understood what I had said and answered: "Oh, but I do not mean that."

"I mean it, but you do not need to write it down, because I have already got my ticket."

"How did you receive it?"

I explained, "About two thousand years ago there was One who bought my ticket for heaven, and I had only to accept it from

Him. That was Jesus when at the Cross He carried my sins and so made the way to heaven free for me."

At that moment a Chinese clerk who had listened to our conversation, passed by. He said, "Yes, that is true." I asked Him: "Have you a reservation in heaven?"

"Yes, I have. I have received Jesus as my Savior and Lord, and He has made me a child of God. And a child of God has a place in heaven in the house of the Father."

I said to him: "Brother, will you see to it that this girl will not be too late with her reservation for a place in heaven."

Then I turned to the girl: "When you do not have a reservation for a seat on a plane, you get into great difficulties, but when you do not have a place in heaven, you will end up in far greater difficulties."

"Brother, you must take care that she is not too late."

Was that a joke? No, I meant it, and I mean it also for you who are reading this. Have you made reservations for a place in heaven? If you are uncertain of your salvation, then make a decision now. "As many as received Him (Jesus) to them gave He power to become the sons of God." (John 1:12)

When the ticket for the journey was ready, the Lord had given me exactly all the money I needed. Thankfully I looked in the booklet with all the different tickets . . . and then I saw the mistake. I phoned the travel agency and asked the girl: "Why have you changed my schedule? My Chief has told me that I must go to Cape Town, after that to Tel Aviv. Now you have changed the sequence, first Tel Aviv and after that Cape Town. God is my Master and I must obey Him."

"But that is impossible," the girl said. "There is not a direct airline from Australia to Africa. There is no island in the Indian Ocean for the plane to land to be refueled. That is why you must first go to Tel Aviv."

'No, I must do what my Chief has told me. Perhaps I must pray for an island in the Indian Ocean? But my schedule has to remain as He told me."

An hour later the girl from the airline phoned: "Did you really pray for an island in the Indian Ocean? I just received a telegram from Qantas, the Australian airline. They have begun to use the Cocoa Islands, and now there is a direct route from Australia to Africa, via the Cocoa Islands and Mauritius."

Corrie replied, "Now you see, Miss, that God does not make mistakes in His plans! There is nothing too great for God's power, and nothing too small for His love."[1]

WHAT WAS CORRIE'S SECRET?

Her long months of suffering and facing death daily while in a concentration camp give much authority to her message. How often she reminded us of our privilege of proving God. It is true, we are usually more conscious of God proving us, that is, testing our motives. But it is equally important for us to know that we have the privilege of proving God. "Prove me ... saith the Lord" (Mal.3:19).

Today, we see how the Lord proved Corrie, but we also see how she proved God, and this perhaps explains her unusual walk with her Lord. As she would insist, "God has a PRIOR CONDITION which we must meet:

> It is our willingness to fully obey God's
> direction that assures us of His help."

There was no doubt in Corrie's mind that God had given her explicit directions about the routing of her ticket. She had learned through the years that her willingness to obey was the PRIOR CONDITION to receiving God's help. Once she had obeyed, then she could rest in the sure confidence that He would intervene, as necessary. It then became His problem! We see how He did this with the airline change.

UNDERSTANDING THE IMPORTANCE OF OUR WILL

All the circumstances of life usually boil down to a governmental issue—God's will and man's will must come into harmony. Is it not interesting that the very word, universe, means one will— and that is what we look forward to when all the purposes of God are finally consummated in His Son, Jesus?

But today we have many wills expressed in the universe. This dischord first started when the arch-enemy of God, Satan, chose an independent course and set up his own will contrary to God's will, and then drew a host of angels with him in the rebellion. This insurrection spread to the Garden when Satan managed to beguile Adam into following him ... i.e. come under his will.

God has now provided redemption through the work of the Lord Jesus on the Cross. The immediate issue is a matter of man's will yielding to God's will—thus bringing rebellious man back under God's government.

When we receive the Lord Jesus as Savior, we are choosing to move from under Satan's government to live under God's government. Paul writes that God has, "... delivered us from the power of darkness, and hath translated us into the kingdom of His dear Son ..."(Col.1:13).

We can see the real importance of exercising our will. In salvation our willingness to come under His lordship was the prior condition—the one thing necessary before God could save us. This initial choice of His Lordship must become our continual choice. Daily as we stand with God and His Word, our continual willingness enables Him to perform His will through us.

Now we move back to Corrie, to see how her willingness to trust that God's schedule was right—even to stand in seeming foolishness—was the prior condition which allowed Him to order new circumstances. Yes, once our choice to stand with God is clearly settled, then His government is free to work mightily.

Corrie explains this more fully. "The devil does his utmost to turn our eyes away from Jesus. He tries to get us so far away that we explain everything by our intellect and argue God's Word. We must never forget that the Bible belongs to the plane of God's 'foolishness'. We can never bring the things of God down to the level of human wisdom, without losing a blessing. But through the Holy Spirit we can bring the wisdom of men up to the higher plane of the 'foolishness' of God. The 'foolishness' of God can only be understood by faith; the wisdom of men through the senses and intellect."[2]

As we look back over the many years in which Corrie walked with unqualified obedience, we must be careful to recognize that she did not learn without some stumbling and pressure. However, she maintained continuous honesty with the Lord. The moment she recognized any unwillingness, she was quick to yield to Him.

HOW WE AVOID FULL OBEDIENCE

Could it be that many people who assume they are walking in full obedience, are not really aware of the "ifs" that qualify their willingness. Let us illustrate some of these:

A man confides, "I would move anywhere to work for the Lord, *but if* He sends me to _____ I could not maintain the quality of life I feel my family deserves...."

Another reasons, "I would get up early each morning to meet the Lord, *but*...it would awaken others in my family...furthermore, I'm not sure about my health...and the Lord knows I need a certain amount of sleep to endure the strain of my job."

A student confesses, "I would _____, *but* other students in school would mock, and I'd become a laughing-stock before them."

A leader sighs, "I would really like to _____ in our church, *but* in spite of what that Bible verse says, it just doesn't seem appropriate for our situation."

Do you recognize the "qualified" obedience? Each is willing to obey, *if* it doesn't conflict with some personal preference, or *if* it doesn't cost too much sacrifice, or *if* it is convenient. Each one seems to be willing, yet it is obvious that self-will is still on the throne. Accepting His lordship in the totality of life is no small thing.

We must be careful lest we re-interpret this PRIOR CONDITION to fit our circumstances. God is looking for our willingness to obey regardless of personal consequences. We can be assured, when God sees such willingness, He is ready to supply all that we may need. Corrie illustrates this again:

"I was in Argentina visiting some patients in a hospital. For the first time in my life I saw polio victims lying in iron lungs. The tragedy so overcame me that I could hardly bear it. A nurse asked me: 'Will you speak with that Jewish man?' He was not in an iron lung, but lay on a bed that went up and down. When his legs went up, his midriff pushed against his lungs and he could breathe out. When his legs went down, he could breathe in. He was fed by a little tube in his nose. He could not speak but he could write.

"When I looked at him I said in despair: 'Oh Lord I cannot do this. Please let me go somewhere else, so that I can cry in a little corner. I am not able to speak to this man.'

"When I say to the Lord, 'I cannot do this,' I always receive the answer, 'I have known that for a long time, but it is good that you know it too, for now you can let Me do it.' And I said, 'Now Lord, then You do it.' And He did! I could speak to this man. I showed him an embroidery, that on one side shows only a tangle of threads, but on the other side a beautiful crown. I said, 'When I see you lying in this bed I think of this embroidery. There was a time in my life when it seemed like the tangled side of this crown. I saw no pattern, no beauty, no harmony. I was in prison where my sister died before my eyes. But all that time I knew that God has no problems, only plans. There is never panic in heaven. Later on I saw God's side of the pattern. Because I have had deep suffering in that prison, I was able to comfort people afterwards . . . .'

"Then I spoke to him about the Messiah, Jesus, the Son of God, who died on the Cross for our sins . . . He will even live in our hearts. We may use His name, and pray in His name. And so I told him the happy message of Jesus' death and life. The man took a piece of paper and wrote: 'I see already the beautiful side of the embroidery of my life.'

"What a victory it was for him to lie there, not being able to move, or speak or breathe, and in spite of all this, to see God's side.

We had a good time together and I was so thankful. I could pray and then thank the Lord with him.

"The next day I went again to the hospital and asked the nurse: 'May I speak with him again?' She told me that he had beckoned her, when I had left, and then wrote on his little writing pad: 'For the first time in my life I have prayed in Jesus' name.' Then he closed his eyes and died. This Jewish man had found Jesus in the last moment of his life. And God had used me for that when I was able to do it. Yes, God's strength is demonstrated in our weakness."[3]

Again we can see how THE PRIOR CONDITION governed in Corrie's life. We see her willingness to obey and trust her Father implicitly brought the help she so much needed.

IN ANOTHER INCIDENT FROM HER LIFE, Corrie reminds us:

The Lord is really a Good Shepherd, and a good shepherd leads His sheep. Yet, again and again I hear Christians say that they do not get any guidance. When we do not know the will of the Lord, the cause is often doubt and disobedience.

Corrie explains: After my time in the concentration camp, all the cruelties of the German Gestapo left such an impression on me. I was so confused that I said to my friends, "I will work anywhere in the world, wherever the Lord sends me, but there is one country where I hope He will never send me, and that is Germany. I never want to hear one word of German again."

That was disobedience. Obedience says, Yes, Father. Disobedience says, Yes, but . . . .

I went to America, and there came a shadow over my prayer life. When I asked God for guidance, I did not get any answer. Then I said, "Lord, why is this? I know that You are my Good Shepherd, so I must be the cause. Have I been disobedient in any way?"

Then the Lord said very clearly, "Germany!" "Then I will go to Germany too, Lord." As soon as I was willing for this, the light came back to my prayer life. I knew at once where the Lord wanted to send me.

THE TESTING CAME

It was in a church in Munich that I saw him, a balding heavy-set man in a gray overcoat, a brown felt hat clutched between his hands. People were filing out of the basement room where I had just spoken, moving along the rows of wooden chairs to the door at the rear ... I had come from Holland to defeated Germany with the message that God forgives.

It was the truth they needed most to hear in that bitter, bombed-out land, and I gave them my favorite mental picture .... The solemn faces stared back at me, not quite daring to believe. There were never questions after a talk in Germany in 1947. People stood in silence ... in silence they left the room.

And that's when I saw him, working his way forward ... one moment I saw the overcoat and the brown hat; the next, a blue uniform and a visored cap with its skull and crossbones. It came back with a rush; the huge room with its harsh overhead lights, the pathetic pile of dresses and shoes in the center of the floor, the shame of walking naked past this man. I could see my sister's frail form ahead of me, ribs sharp beneath the parchment skin. Betsie, how thin you were!

Now he was in front of me, hand thrust out, "A fine message, Fraulein! How good it is to know that, as you say, all our sins are at the bottom of the sea!"

And I who had spoken so glibly of forgiveness, fumbled at my pocketbook rather than take that hand. He would not remember me, of course. How could he remember one prisoner among those thousands of women?

But I remembered him and the leather crop swinging from his belt. It was the first time since my release that I had been face to face with one of my captors, and my blood seemed to freeze. ·

"You mentioned Ravensbruk in your talk," he was saying. "I was a guard in there." No, he did not remember me.

"But since that time," he went on, "I have become a Christian. I know that God has forgiven me for the cruel things I did there, but I would like to hear it from your lips as well. "Fraulein,"– again the hand went out—"will you forgive me?"

And I stood there—I whose sins had every day to be forgiven—and could not. Betsie had died in that place; could he erase her slow terrible death simply for the asking?

It could not have been many seconds that he stood there, hand held out, but to me it seemed hours as I wrestled with the most difficult thing I had ever had to do.

ᶜ   For I had to do it—I knew that. The message that God forgives has a PRIOR CONDITION: that we forgive those who have injured us. "If you do not forgive men their trespasses," Jesus says, "neither will your Father in heaven forgive your tresspasses."

I knew it not only as a commandment of God, but as a daily experience. Since the end of the war I had had a home in Holland for victims of Nazi brutality. Those who were able to forgive their former enemies were able also to return to the outside world and rebuild their lives, no matter what the physical scars. Those who nursed their bitterness remained invalids. It was as simple and as horrible as that.

And still I stood there with the coldness clutching my heart. But forgiveness is not an emotion—I knew that too. Forgiveness is an act of the will, and the will can function regardless of the temperature of the heart. Jesus, help me! I prayed silently. I can lift my hand. I can do that much. You supply the feeling.

And so woodenly, mechanically, I thrust my hand into the one stretched out to me. And as I did, an incredible thing took place. The current started in my shoulder, raced down my arm, sprang into our joined hands. And then this healing warmth seemed to flood my whole being, bringing tears to my eyes.

"I forgive you, brother!" I cried. "With all my heart!"

For a long moment we grasped each other's hands, the former guard and the former prisoner. I had never known God's love so intensely as I did at that moment.

> Forgiveness is the key which unlocks the door of resentment and the handcuffs of hatred. It breaks the chains of bitterness and the shackles of selfishness."[4]

QUICKENING FROM GOD'S WORD

I hope we shall never forget: our willingness to lay aside all vain reasonings allows God to perform His work in and through us. When Paul says, "For me to will is present . . . how to perform . . ." he is explaining, that as we set our will, God can do the performing, which we could never do. (Rom.7:18)

Again, when Paul writes, ". . . if we have first a willing mind, it is accepted . . . " he is saying that God waits for our choice before He is free to perform.(2 Cor.8:12)

For this reason Paul could testify, "I can do all things through Christ, who strengthens me . . ." (Phil.4:13)

AWAKEN MY HEART to my need for continual willingness.

Father, I do want to be more consistent in my willingness to obey, as I have seen in Corrie. Surely it was this one condition that allowed You to work through her so mightily. I long for the same! I realize anew that there are no shortcuts to recognizing Your voice. It only comes through much fellowship—much quiet listening!

I also recognize how often my analyzing mind has risen up to question whether it was Your voice I was hearing, or just my own impressions. You keep reminding me there is only one way to discern these "ifs" and "buts" that crowd into my analyzing mind. Through spending more time in fellowship I can recognize the distinctiveness of Your voice.

I recall how one who walked with You for many years whispered in my ear years ago, "You need to saturate yourself in God's Word, and you will then recognize the quality of His voice; you need to meet Him early while the dew is still on the grass, and you will then be more attentive to His slightest wish." Lord, how slow I have been. How patient You have been. It has taken all these years for me to appreciate the wisdom in this counsel. I do want to finish my days, like Corrie, alive to You and sensitive to Your slightest wish. Then with . . .

OVERFLOWING GRATITUDE . . . I can sing

> When we walk with the Lord,
>   In the light of His Word
> What a glory He sheds on our way!
>   While we do His good will
> He abides with us still,
>   And with all who will trust and obey.
>
>> Trust and Obey,
>> For there's no other way
>> To be happy in Jesus,
>> But to trust and obey.
>
> But we never can prove
>   The delights of His love
> Until all on the altar we lay;
>   For the favor He shows,
> And the joy He bestows,
>   Are for those who will trust and obey.
>
> Then in fellowship sweet
>   We will sit at His feet,

Or we'll walk by His side in the way;
What He says we will do,
Where He sends we will go—
Never fear, only trust and obey.
(Daniel B. Towner)

PRAYER REQUESTS   DATE ANSWERED

_____
_____
_____
_____
_____
_____
_____
_____
_____
_____
_____
_____
_____
_____
_____
_____
_____
_____
_____
_____

INSIGHTS FROM LESSON

_____
_____
_____
_____
_____
_____
_____
_____
_____
_____
_____

DAY TEN

WHEN THE PRESSURES OF LIFE seem unbearable, you don't need to accept the three "D's": discouragement, depression, despair. Though circumstances may crowd you until there seems to be no way out, God has THE WAY, as we shall see in this lesson.

Sooner or later everyone of us will need to personally experience the reality of this verse: "...lay aside every encumbrance...and let us run with endurance the race that is set before us, FIXING OUR EYES ON JESUS..." (Heb.12:1 NAS).

IN OUR LESSON...we consider the difference between:

> the *fixation* of the soul, and
> the *proper gaze* of our heart.

How often we are captured by circumstances or "impossible" people. We allow our mind and emotions to become glued to them—and our soul develops a fixation. Multitudes in the world, and too many in God's own family, become victims of this kind of captivity—or fixation. There is help! But we must offer more than a "mental gymnastic"; we must offer God's way to victory. We shall see what that is today.

HERE ARE THE TESTIMONIES of six well-known saints, whose experiences of life's TRUE OCCUPATION gives them authority to speak to us. Read carefully and be encouraged.

My True Occupation.

DOWN THROUGH THE CENTURIES many triumphant saints have used the phrase, *"proper gaze of our heart."* What did they really mean? In seeking to explain this, Gordon Allport insists that "what gains and sustains our attention will ultimately change our lives."

Let us consider the testimony of several who learned to fix the eyes of their heart upon the Lord, instead of allowing the fixation of their soul to be upon the disturbing things of this world.

We must understand that this turning from soul-fixation to heart-gaze is more than a psychological diversion. The primary ministry of the Holy Spirit is to keep us continually occupied with our Lord Jesus, thus this turning is accomplished. It is true that we can learn the mental gymnastics of turning our attention from one thing to another, but while this diversion may seem helpful, it is only temporary. The fixation of our soul upon problems will only bring frustration, while the gaze of our heart upon the Lord will allow us to more clearly perceive spiritual realities.

Life's experiences will finally lead us to this conclusion:

If our *gaze* is continually upon the Lord Jesus,
we need only *glance* at all else.

In his excellent prayer manual, Peter Lord further amplifies this thought. "If we allow our gaze to be on our request, it will dominate our prayers. We will tell God what we see and what needs to be done. However, if our gaze is upon God, we will ask Him to interpret the situation from His viewpoint (that is, tell us what He sees) and tell us what He wants done."[1]

CORRIE FOUND THIS SECRET.

She explains how the Lord became the focus of her heart-gaze when she was in a concentration camp during World War II:

We had to stand every day for two or three hours for roll-call, often in icy-cold wind. That was something terrible, but even worse, once a woman guard used these hours to demonstrate her cruelty. I could hardly bear to see and hear what happened in front of me. Then God had His lovely way.

Suddenly a skylark started to sing high in the sky. We all looked up, and when I looked to the sky and listened to its song, I looked still higher and thought of the verse: "For the heavens are high above the earth, so great is His steadfast love toward those who fear Him" (Ps.103:11 RSV).

Suddenly I realized that this love of God was a greater reality than any cruelty that I could experience or that I saw around me. "Oh the love of God; how deep and great, far deeper than man's deepest hate."

And you know! God sent that skylark every day for three weeks, just at the time of roll-call, to give us an opportunity to turn our eyes away from the cruelty of man to the ocean of God's love. This love is a protection as well as a weapon. It guards us against impatience, against zeal without sense, against annoyance, against bitterness, against gloating. It is a very strong weapon in the battle to win souls, for it never gives in.[2]

MARTIN LUTHER LEARNS TO KEEP HIS EYES ON JESUS.

This 16th century reformer tells how he overcame depressing doubts. On one such occasion a friend said to Luther, "Our Lord in heaven is looking down and probably thinking, 'What shall I do with this man Luther? I have poured My mercies upon him and given him many gifts and much grace, and yet he will despair of My goodness.' " These well-chosen words shook Luther out of his gloom and uncertainty.

Later, when another friend visited Luther to complain about how severely the devil was buffeting him, Luther told his visitor, "The devil can do that in a masterly way; otherwise he would be no devil. You come to me, dear friend, and believe that I can surely comfort you through God's Word, and that is good. But if you expect good from me, what may you not expect from Christ who died for you? Look up to Him who is ten thousand times better than I." Out of his own struggle and failure, Luther had found that to dispel doubt and keep above despair, he had to keep his eyes on the Lord.

Years ago I wrote this warning in the back of my Bible. "You'll be upset if you look at people too much. If you look around, you'll be distracted; if you look within yourself, you'll be discouraged; only as you keep looking unto Jesus will you develop confidence and peace." Again and again as I have turned to this page, these words have helped me to keep my heart gaze upon the only One who guarantees peace.

"Thou wilt keep him in perfect peace, whose mind is stayed on thee, because he trusteth in thee" (Isa.26:3).

A MOTHER FOUND THE TRUE OCCUPATION

The late Robert Mc Quilken, while president of Columbia Bible College, relates: A dear Christian mother came to me at the close of a meeting, and with troubled face and voice cried, "Oh for that life of victory! That is what I need." She then poured out her story of the trouble in her home because of the unworthy conduct of a young man who had married her beautiful daughter.

"Have you ever read the 37th Psalm?" I asked.

Her face lighted up. "That is my favorite psalm. I know it by heart."

"What is the first word of that psalm?" I asked. I expected her to say, 'Fret not.' She answered accurately, 'Fret.'

Would you believe that was the only part of the 37th Psalm she knew in experience? Why? She was fretting much of the time. She repeated the first sentence of the psalm, "Fret not thyself because of evil doers." I asked her who was fretting her? She said it was the young man, and proceeded to tell other things about the troubles in their home.

After repeating the three opening words of this 37th Psalm several times, the meaning of the words "Fret not THYSELF" finally dawned upon her.

"Oh," she cried, "you mean that I'm the one that's doing it, and all the time I thought it was that man."

"Yes, others may be the occasion of our worry, but no one can fret us except we ourselves."

Years afterward I heard the good news. That mother learned that day the secret of the peace that passeth understanding. Moreover, the son-in-law became an earnest, useful Christian, and theirs became a joyful, happy home." (3)

You will notice in this psalm that those little words, fret not, occur three times, and each time they are followed by that other word, "thyself," showing clearly that it is an injury we inflict upon ourselves.

Consider how much our fretting is like a fret-saw, which looks very innocent, yet can do much damage to a piece of hardwood. We would never think of using a fret-saw on the flesh of our arm. Yet how apt we are to allow our fretting to "cut away" on our delicate mind and spirit.

When reading this psalm, usually our attention is turned to the beginning words: trust, delight, commit, rest, and wait. However these words are simply arrows that point to the provision:

Trust—IN THE LORD.
Delight thyself—IN THE LORD.
Commit thy way—UNTO THE LORD.
Trust also—IN THE LORD.
Rest—IN THE LORD.
Wait patiently—FOR HIM.

What Dr. Mc Quilken saw in this mother was a soul-fixation. Her attention was glued to her problem son-in-law. Only as she deliberately turned her heart toward the Lord was she enabled to turn from "fretting herself".

Who has not been guilty of this fretting? At some time we have experienced lying awake in the silent hours of the night, reflecting on how someone has wronged us, or on how some circumstance is limiting us, or pondering on some past blunder or some grievous sin, though long ago confessed and forgiven—yet fixes itself on our minds so as to allow the cruel work of fretting.

DR. F.B. MEYER FOUND GOD'S WAY

This world-famous servant of God confessed that when he was young, he was very irritable. One day an old saint told him how he had found relief from this very thing by looking up the moment he felt the irritation coming, and saying: "Thy sweetness, Lord." In sharing this with him, that discerning man greatly helped Dr. Meyer, who then began to share it with tens of thousands wherever he went.

He explained: Take the opposite attitude. If there has been untruth, plead, Thy truth, Lord; unkindness—Thy kindness, Lord; Impatience—Thy patience, Lord; Selfishness—Thy unselfishness, Lord; Roughness—Thy gentleness, Lord; Discourtesy—Thy courtesy, Lord; Resentment, inward heat, fuss—Thy sweetness, Lord, Thy calmness, Thy peacefulness.

In referring to this practice of becoming occupied with the Lord, Amy Carmichael confides, "I think that no one who tries this very simple plan will ever give it up. Will all to whom this is new try it for a day, a week, a month?"

It should be very clear to us that God has just one real answer to all our problems:

TOTAL OCCUPATION WITH HIS LOVELY SON.

His Son, Jesus, is to be the very center and source of our living. In His own way, as we are rightly occupied with Him, God is at liberty to operate on our problems. "Do not be anxious about anything, but in everything, by prayer and petition, with thanksgiving, present your requests to God. And the peace of God, which transcends all understanding, will guard your hearts and your minds in Christ Jesus" (Phil.4:6-7).

I can almost hear someone asking, "Does this mean if we ignore our problems, they will go away?" On occasion that may happen, but that is not God's solution. In turning our heart to gaze upon the Lord, we are—so to speak—granting Him permission to adjust and correct whatever He sees to be out of line with His purpose.

DR. A.W.TOZER TELLS OF HIS PURSUIT

Those who knew him and enjoyed his unique ministry will recall how he insisted that, "Faith is our gaze upon a saving God. It is not a once-done act, but the continuous gaze of the heart at the triune God.

"While we are looking at God we do not see ourselves—blessed riddance. The man who has struggled to purify himself and has had nothing but repeated failures will experience real relief when he stops tinkering with his soul and looks away to the Perfect One. While he looks at Christ, the very things he has so long been trying to do will be getting done within him. It will be God working in him to will and to do.

"When the habit of inwardly gazing Godward becomes fixed within us, we shall be ushered into a new level of spiritual life more in keeping with the promises of God and the mood of the New Testament. The triune God will be our dwelling place even while our feet walk the low road of simple duty here among men. We will have found life's summum bonum indeed."

EVEN JACOB FOUND THE WAY

After Jacob's memorable encounter with God he built an altar which he called Beth-el, meaning the house of God. (Gen.35:1)

Some time later, having discovered the emptiness of all earthly things, and having been conquered and blessed by God —in an hour of spiritual agony—he renamed the place El-beth-el, which means "the God of the house of God." (Gen.35:7) Historically the place was always known as *Beth-el*, but in Jacob's awakened heart it was now to be *El-beth-el*.

The change is significant. Jacob had shifted his emphasis from *the house*, to *the One* whom he met there. God Himself now took the center of his interest. He had at last been "converted" from a place to God Himself. A most blessed conversion!

Many Christians never get beyond serving the cause, the project, the "thing" they are developing for God. God is in their thoughts, but He is not first. Somehow their building the house of God (Bethel) has become first. There has been no intention for this to happen, yet unwittingly that good thing they are building for God has come to eclipse Him.

Perhaps there is someone reading this who has unknowingly allowed some good "cause" to take center stage. I know! For years I labored to produce a spiritual house for God: Bethel was my goal. Yet instead of a house I saw only scattered piles of living stones here and there. What frustration to "see" and yet not produce! The more determined I was to produce a Bethel for God, the more illusive it became. Then . . . . one day He showed me the altar at El-beth-el. That day I returned to my TRUE OCCUPATION, putting God first and His house second. For the first time those words of Jesus took on new meaning: "I will build my church . . . ." I knew Him as my *Life* and as the *Truth*, but He was also to become *THE WAY*.

TOZER EXPLAINS THE BALANCE

"Faithfulness to the local church is a good thing. The true Christian will, by a kind of spiritual instinct, find a body of believers somewhere, identify himself with it and try by every proper means to promote its growth and prosperity. And that, we repeat, is good. But when the church becomes so large and important that it hides God from our eyes, it is no longer a good thing. Or better say that it is a good thing wrongly used. For the church was never intended to substitute for God. Let us understand that as every local church embraces El-beth-el, the right balance will be found and maintained: God first and His house second."

Finally, we must see that all things— problems, pressures, people, circumstances, conditions, even worthwhile causes—all must be evicted from center-stage, or we will develop a soul-fixation. We can judge our spiritual growth pretty accurately by observing the total emphasis of our heart-gaze. Where is my primary interest? Is it Beth-el or El-beth-el? Is it my church or my Lord? Is it my ministry or my God? My creed or my Christ? My healing or my Healer? My blessed experience or my Blesser? We are spiritual or carnal just as we are pre-occupied with the "house" or with our TRUE OCCUPATION: the God of the house.

QUICKENING FROM GOD'S WORD

We are sure that David had discovered the Lord as his TRUE OCCUPATION , for he writes, "The one thing I want from God, the thing I seek most of all, is the privilege of meditating in His Temple, living in His presence every day of my life, delighting in His incomparable perfections and glory.

"There I'll be when troubles come. He will hide me. He will set me on a rock out of reach of all my enemies. Then I will bring Him sacrifices and sing His praises with much joy. Listen to my pleading, Lord! Be merciful and send the help I need.

"My heart has heard you say, 'Come and talk with me, O my people.' And my heart responds, 'LORD, I AM COMING' " (Ps.27 L.B.).

AWAKEN MY HEART .... to be occupied with YOU.

Thank You, my Father! New light is breaking through. I see how keeping my focus on circumstances, on people, on myself has only drained my energy and destroyed true perception. Forgive me! I now realize that You have tried to turn my attention away from these soul-fixations that have captured me, but I was not ready. Now I know that You alone can be the "Turner of my captivity."

With the psalmist David I will also announce that You alone are worthy of my continual gaze—You shall be my TRUE OCCUPATION. In beholding You I will trust, delight, commit, rest and wait instead of fret.

My heart is filled with thanksgiving as I realize how long You have been working in areas where I needed emotional freedom. I am grateful that You are even now taking care of many things—because You are allowed to work in Your own time and way. Indeed I am learning what it means to fellowship with You and not fellowship my problems.

I look back almost forty years ago, when as a result of a terrible accident I lay on my hospital bed, eyes covered with bandages—wondering what it would be like to finish my race without eyesight. In my hour of great need it was surely You who prompted Helen Lemmel to send her friend with a special word and a song of encouragement for me. This friend, who had traveled 150 miles to my hospital room, told me Helen had been blind throughout most of her life, yet had continually enjoyed "seeing" You with the eyes of her heart. She also explained how You had given Helen inner eyes to behold Your beauty and she had written a song which all Your children have come to love. Then as she placed in my hands an autographed copy of TURN YOUR EYES UPON JESUS, she sang it for me. Though I could not see her, I shall never forget the assurance that came to me in that moment:

> *I would again see with my physical eyes and even*
> *more, He would also answer my longing to see, as*
> *Helen, with the eyes of my heart.*

OVERFLOWING GRATITUDE: (If you love this song as I do, please get your book and sing it with me.)

> Turn your eyes upon Jesus,
> Look full in His wonderful face,
> And the things of earth
>   Will grow strangely dim,
> In the light of His glory and grace.
>   O soul, are you weary and troubled?
>   No light in the darkness you see?
>   There's light for a LOOK AT THE SAVIOR,
>   And life more abundant and free.
>   (Helen Lemmel)

PRAYER REQUESTS   DATE ANSWERED

_____
_____
_____
_____
_____
_____
_____
_____
_____
_____
_____
_____
_____
_____
_____
_____
_____
_____
_____
_____

INSIGHTS FROM LESSON

_____
_____
_____
_____
_____
_____
_____
_____
_____
_____
_____
_____
_____
_____
_____
_____
_____
_____
_____
_____

DAY ELEVEN

SURELY ONE OF THE MORE DIFFICULT QUESTIONS we all face is, why do God's children suffer? If we are spiritual enough, can we not expect to avoid all trouble? The answer is no! But we can, through fellowship with God, better understand His ways. We know our Lord Jesus learned obedience by the things He suffered; can we expect less?

Since our face is set to finish life's race triumphantly, we will press on—even though it may mean going through some testing disciplines in life. Today we shall learn a most blessed secret: How to avail ouselves of God's rich supply of grace—so as not to become offended when we encounter hardships.

TROUBLE OR TESTING is not necessarily a sign of sin or failure, or lack of spirituality. As we have already seen, God's ways to prepare us for special ministry are varied. In this lesson we see how in a time of testing one man reacts negatively, while another responds properly. We see how one becomes hardened, and the other becomes mellow and teachable.

IN OUR STORY John Wright Follette shares an intimate story of his responding to God in a time of difficulty. Mr. Follette was one of the early pioneers in the ways of the Spirit. I shall forever be grateful to God that he crossed my pathway during a most formative time in my spiritual walk, and the wise counsel I received from him helped me make a proper choice at a critical juncture.

Reacting or Responding

JOHN WRIGHT FOLLETTE writes: I want to share a personal experience which may be of help to some who are anxious over the welfare of loved ones. I remember very well when as a lad of sixteen—a very trying period for young lives when important decisions are made and the first steps are taken which often determine the destiny of a life—tragedy came into our happy home.

Out of a clear sky, in no way the fault of those of whom I speak, great trouble cast a shadow over our family. My father was a Christian, a member of the church and had a fine moral character. But his faith in the experimental matters of the daily life was weak. He could not see God in the matter and so turned away from the whole idea of God, or the thought of trusting Him. His human reasoning got the better of him and plunged him into unbelief and bitterness. He made no great outward fuss; in fact, he said very little. But his few remarks told us his attitude. He dropped his church life, ceased to say grace at the table, and had absolutely no interest in the things of God. He knew he was not to blame and so naturally reasoned,

"Why has such trouble come?"

After we live long enough we learn that trouble does not come always because we are to blame, but when it does come, we should interpret it in God's light and cause it to serve us. It may be one of the greatest teachers to instruct and discipline us. I was a lad in high school and a worldly Christian, a member of the church but without any vital touch with God. I do not relate this to show I had

115

more faith or was any better than my father. I want simply to show you how the same trouble may work differently on hearts....

The trouble kept me pressed into God. For eighteen years Father was still bitter in heart, though to us as a family he was kind and a good father. He provided for us and was interested in our welfare. But I knew all the time he carried in his poor, dear heart a great hurt. No human could help him and he would not let God, so he bore it in silence.

During those eighteen years in which he was a backslider, naturally I tried to help him. But I soon learned a great lesson—the difference between my way, and God's way. I had to take the usual criticism of interested friends... I had to keep my hands off whether people understood or not, and so to many I seemed indifferent to my dear father's need. I prayed through and committed him to God. After that I was not indifferent but restful. Faith is not indifference, unconcern, and apathy. It is most vital attention held in profound rest and assurance. I knew God would take care of him in His own time and way.

It was eighteen years later in June... I went home for a few days and found Father quite broken in health and unable to continue his business. He was up and around, but able to go for only a short walk each day.

One day when I knew mother was out shopping and I thought Father was out walking, I sat down at the piano and began to sing. I felt I needed a little refreshing from the Spirit. As I sat there I sang, "God Will Take Care of You." Then I felt to sing it again and even a third time. The Spirit was there and I felt His sweet presence.

I was thirsty and so stepped out to the kitchen for a drink of water. To my utter surprise, there sat Father in tears. I did not know he was in the house. I shall never forget the pathetic look in his eyes as he buried his face against me. All he could do was to draw close (oh, so close) and press his face against me. He was all broken to pieces and between sobs said,

"Dad wants to hear it now.
Yes, talk to me; I want to hear it."

No need to tell you God was there! We had a most blessed time. It was God's time, and I had nothing to do with it. God brought him wonderfully to a new place by His side. Father broke and opened to God like a crushed and broken flower, one that had not given its beauty and fragrance to the world, but which now needed the light and warmth of the sun and had found it. He just seemed to drink God in to his thirsty soul.

A few days later he suffered a stroke and went to his death-bed. He stayed only a few days. The pull from the other side was too great and he kept saying, "Oh, let me go! I want to go." The day before he slipped away, he spoke to us all about the things of God. He quoted Scripture verses I never knew he had in his head or heart. Then while resting upon my arm on his pillow, he went home.

Have you met tragedy? Do you have dear ones who are yet unsaved or backslidden? How are you interpreting your trouble? Can you trace God's fingers in the outline? Do not try to reason it out. Pray it through! Run to God and bury your tired head upon His breast. Lean hard! Lean hard! Those eighteen years were long, but full of God. Our little natural interest and help never get us any-where. Put the loved ones and backsliders into God's hands and let Him work out the problem. Faith is not indifference; it is most wonderfully keen and awake, yet restful, and can even sing."[1]

THE DIFFERENCE BETWEEN REACTING AND RESPONDING

No one can ever know the inward struggles and reasonings of the heart during such a testing time as John and his father faced. Even without knowing the inner hurts and wounds, we can recognize the difference between REACTING and RESPONDING. In react-ing, our soul becomes bitter and unteachable; in responding, our spirit can take from the river of God's grace.

In Scripture we learn that we as children of God are like trees planted with a river of grace flowing deep within reach of our roots. (Ps.1) This means whenever we encounter some bitter trial, hardship, misunderstanding or tragedy, we can either receive God's grace or resist God's grace.

As we have pictured, to resist is to turn one's roots upward in pride and self-will; to receive is to humble oneself under the hand of God and allow our roots to go down to drink of the river of His grace. Sooner or later all of us will have this opportunity to receive or resist. We must remember, it is not if the storms of life come, but when they come. No one is exempt, whether of the world or as a child in God's family. However, we have this good news—God's grace is available to all.

Just what is this grace of which we may so freely drink?

Grace is the desire and power that God gives to help us respond to every life-situation according to His will.

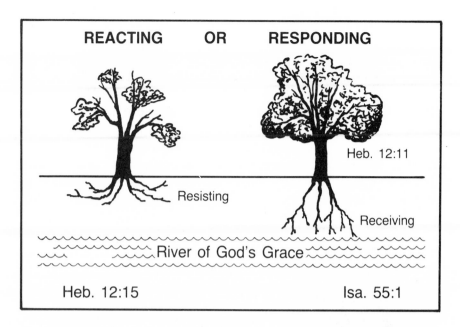

REACTING OR RESPONDING

Heb. 12:11

Resisting

Receiving

River of God's Grace

Heb. 12:15   Isa. 55:1

Let no one complain that this river of grace is not available to all of God's children. In this, God is no respector of persons. His invitation is open to all. Let everyone come and drink freely of His supply. (Isa.55:1)

When trouble came to the Follette home, we see how John's father reacted in his soul: Pride, self-will and unteachableness turned his roots up. Because of reacting he suffered unnecessarily all those years. But we also see how John Wright properly responded to God, and his roots moved down to drink deeply (receive) from the river of God's grace.

It is alarming that many of God's children live in the illusion that they are to be immune from the pressures and hardships which are common to all. Throughout the Bible, it is clearly evident that the center of God's will is never marked by outward ease and comfort. None escaped the storms of life. Should we consider ourselves more fortunate than those early apostles who were imprisoned and beaten for their faith, yet rejoiced that they were counted worthy to suffer shame for His name. Should we today expect anything less?

IT IS EASY TO BE OFFENDED, UNLESS . . .

Let us look at John the Baptist. From his prison cell he hears about the mighty works Jesus is doing, so he sends two of his disciples to ask certain questions. We can understand why John might be puzzled. Here he is, suffering in prison, and seems to be ignored by Jesus, with the majority of his disciples taken over by

Him. John's expectations are shaken as to whether Jesus is really the long-anticipated Messiah of Israel. It is no wonder that John asks, "Are You really the One—or should we look for Another?"

If anyone ever had a right to be offended or disillusioned, it would seem John had that right. Yet we must be careful: John may have had a "reason", (reasoning from his point of view) but he had no right. Why? Like each of us, John needed simply to direct his own roots down to take from God's river of grace. Instead of reacting to his circumstances, John must respond to God's available grace. Perhaps what should stand out to us is that in replying to John's inner agony, Jesus simply sends these words: "Blessed is he, who shall not be OFFENDED in me" (Matt.11:6).

A few weeks later when Jesus was teaching His disciples, He seemed to say again, If any of you can be offended, sooner or later it will happen. ". . . He that received the seed into stony places, the same is he that heareth the word, and with joy receiveth it; yet hath he not root in himself, but endureth for a while: for when tribulation or persecution ariseth because of the word, he is OFFENDED" (Matt.13:20 21).

A bit later in His home town of Nazareth there was much jealousy and vain reasoning. ". . . Whence hath this man this wisdom, and these mighty works? Is not this the carpenter's son? Is not his mother called Mary? And his brethren, James and Joses, and Simon and Judas? And his sisters, are they not all with us? Whence then hath this man all these things? AND THEY WERE OFFENDED IN HIM" (Matt. 13:54-57).

Yes, down through the centuries to this very hour, men have been offended with God because they could not understand or accept His ways. And yet to those with open hearts (broken and contrite spirits) He eagerly waits to reveal Himself and His ways. Some who are offended react, and their roots resist His grace and turn up; others are responsive to God in their crisis and allow their roots to go down to His river of grace. We need to be careful about our "root-life."

WHAT IS YOUR PREVAILING ATTITUDE?

While it is necessary to recognize "fallen man's" proneness to be offended and react toward life's reverses, it is more important that God's children know how to respond with a healthy attitude. Consider the following contrasts:

The world sees disaster and interprets it as TRAGEDY;
The Christian sees it and expects His God to TRIUMPH!

The worldling struggles because he is always a VICTIM;
 The believer, rooted in God, knows he is always a VICTOR!

No one can interpret life's troubles without becoming CYNICAL;
 Except the child of God who knows who he is—and is CONFIDENT!

Sooner or later life's reverses tempt everyone to be OFFENDED;
 Yet the one established in God knows how to be an OVERCOMER!

 What is your prevailing mind-set? We soon recognize that all the "negativism of the fall" will surface unless we have learned to keep our hearts nourished in Him. In the closing hour of the persent age, God is determined to "shake everything that can be shaken" that we might be established in Him. (Jam.5:5,8)

 THE CHRISTIAN ATTITUDE HAS ALWAYS BEEN one of victory and triumph. It is THE WAY God designed. There is no pain, no suffering, no frustration, no disappointment that cannot be cured or taken up and used for higher ends. You can take up everything (except sin) into the purpose of your life and make it contribute to the rest of life.

 Throughout God's Word we see how many were able to face deep trouble and hurt as they turned to God and experienced His faithfulness. As encouragement, let us record some we recognize:

Read	Their problem	Their prayer
Genesis 45: 1-8		
Job 1:13-22;42:1,2,10		
1 Sam. 30:1-8		
Acts 16:19-32		

 It is noteworthy that the Judeo/Christian way is uniquely different from all religions. For example, Hinduism and Buddhism attempt to explain everything, and leave everything as before. THE WAY explains little and yet changes everything in sight, for its answer is not verbal; it is a vital answer.

 We have been seeing how life is determined more by reactions than by actions. Life comes to you without your acting, it forces situations upon you without your asking or acting. It is then that your reacting or responding counts. You can react in self-pity and in frustration. Or you can respond with confidence and courage, allowing the pressure to make you better. Its origin may be evil, but by the time it gets through to you—you have turned it into good.

TESTIMONIES OF THOSE WHO RESPONDED TO GRACE

A woman of culture surrendered herself to God, and then troubles began to pile in: her husband began "wandering", and her daughter, a brilliant girl, went to a mental hospital. She brought them both back through her responsiveness to God. The daughter, restored by her mother's love and faith, said: "Mother, everything is poured on you. You get over one thing, and then its another. But you sit there and smile. You're wonderful." She was—for she was *rooted* and *responding*! This is how she summed it up: "Nothing hurts me now. I have power to come back from anything." Her teeth were falling out; the dentist said nothing could be done. She surrendered the matter to God, prayed and her teeth tightened up. "You'll die with them," said the dentist in astonishment, as he described how tight they were. It was this woman's continual RESPONDING TO GOD that made all kinds of weather serve her.

Edwin Markham says: "sorrow stretches our hearts for joy." It does, and more—it stretches our hearts for new communion *with Him*, and new usefulness *for Him*. Sorrow plows the field for God's sowing and our harvest.

During those dark days of the holocaust, an eminent Jewish doctor was standing naked and stripped before the Gestapo. They had taken his watch and then had seen his gold wedding band and demanded it as well. As he took the wedding band off his finger to hand it to the Gestapo officer, a thought went through his mind. He said to his captors: "There is one thing you can never take from me and that is my freedom to choose how I will react to whatever you do to me!" He was refusing to allow his soul to react to their inhumanity. Instead his would be a response to the available supply of grace.

A young Armenian nurse and her brother had been attacked by Turks in a lane, and while she had escaped by climbing over a wall, her brother had been brutally killed before her eyes. Later on while nursing in the hospital, she recognized one of her patients as the very Turkish soldier who had murdered her brother. Her first reaction was to get revenge. He was very ill, just hovering between life and death. The slightest neglect, and he would die. No one would ever know! His life was absolutely in her hands. But instead of revenge she decided for Christ's sake to forgive him. She fought for his life and won, nursing him back to health—only because her roots reached down to receive from His grace.

Later while he was convalescing, she told him who she was. The Turkish soldier looked at her in astonishment and asked,

"Then why didn't you let me die, when you had me in your power?" "I couldn't," was her answer. "I just couldn't, for I am a Christian, and my own Master forgave His enemies who crucified Him. I must do the same, for His sake." "Well," said the hardened Turk in astonishment, "if that is what it means to be a Christian, I want to be one."

Many who have appreciated the writings of Andrew Murray on prayer and fellowship with God will be amazed to discover that he was not always the spiritual giant as known in his later years. In giving his own testimony he explains how something very painful happened which moved him to the very edge of being offended with God. In that most trying moment he waited silently before His Lord, and then wrote these words for himself:

First, He brought me here; it is by His will I am in this strait place; in that fact I will rest.

Next, He will keep me here in His love, and give me grace to behave as His child.

Then, He will make the trial a blessing, teaching me the lessons He intends me to learn, and working in me the grace He means to bestow.

Last, in His good time He can bring me out again—how and when He knows. Let me say I am here,

(1) By God's appointment
(2) In His keeping
(3) Under His training,
(4) For His time."

QUICKENING FROM GOD'S WORD

Hear these words of David when he is surrounded by troubles: "But when I am afraid, I will put my confidence in You, Yes, I will trust the promises of God. And since I am trusting him, what can mere man do to me? They are always twisting what I say. All their thoughts are how to harm me. They meet together to perfect their plans . . . .

"You have seen me tossing and turning through the night. You have collected all my tears and preserved them in your bottle! You have recorded every one in your book.

"The very day I call for help, the tide of battle turns. My enemies flee! This one thing I know: God is for me! I am trusting God—oh, praise his promises. I am not afraid of anything mere man can do to me! . . . For you have saved me from death and my feet from slipping, so that I can walk before the Lord in the land of the living" (Psa.56 L.B.).

AWAKEN MY HEART to always respond rightly . . . to You

Lord, I do not want to allow any hidden roots of bitterness to limit my fellowship; please uncover and expose whatever You may see—that I have missed. I do want the remaining years left to me to be full and triumphant. I thank You for all I now enjoy of Your presence, yet somehow, I long for an even deeper measure of fellowship. I do not want to be satisfied with crumbs, when You would offer the whole loaf. Nor do I want fellowship just for my joy alone, but also for Your pleasure. Thank You! I know You hear and will work this out.

OVERFLOWING GRATITUDE

You have noticed, I am sure, that the early Christians were always singing. Even when cast into jail or thrown to the wild beasts in the arena, they met their hour with a faith that expressed itself in song. The last act of Jesus before leaving the upper room to go out into the darkness of His arrest and crucifixion, was to join His friends in a hymn. Imagine! Singing as you move toward death! He belonged to what someone has called THE FELLOWSHIP OF SINGING HEARTS.

Through the centuries we recall how many of the saints were always singing. John and Charles Wesley, Martin Luther, Isaac Watts, John G. Whittier, and countless others have enriched our spiritual heritage with their hymns. If you have not given yourself to an appreciation of this vast treasure, I would plead with you. Begin now! Join the choir of those who know how to release their spirit in praise and thanksgiving.

Though it was many years ago, I can still see my friend John Wright Follette sitting at his piano, releasing his spirit in song to the Lord he loved so much. If you have wondered why we close each day with the words of a hymn or praise chorus, it is to encourage you to blend your voice with that vast choir of God's children who are now tuning up—getting prepared for the ages to come. With John Follette, let us all sing:

Be not dismayed what-e'er betide,
    God will take care of you!
Beneath His wings of love abide,

God will take care of you!
    God will take care of you,
    Through ev'ry day o'er all the way;
    He will take care of you;
    God will take care of you!

All you may need He will provide,
    God will take care of you!
Trust Him, and you will be satisfied,
    God will take care of you!

Lonely and sad, from friends apart,
    God will take care of you!
He will give peace to your aching heart,
    God will take care of you!

No matter what may be the test,
    God will take care of you!
Lean, weary one, upon His breast,
    God will take care of you!
                    (C.D. Martin)

PRAYER REQUESTS   DATE ANSWERED

_____
_____
_____
_____
_____
_____
_____
_____
_____
_____
_____

INSIGHTS FROM LESSON

_____
_____
_____
_____
_____
_____
_____
_____
_____
_____

DAY TWELVE

I REALLY NEED TO ASK MYSELF—am I being driven to prayer by circumstances, or being drawn by desire to fellowship with God. If I am really honest about my motive, I guess I would admit to a bit of both.

In a world whose keynote is utility, the significance of prayer-fellowship is generally judged from the visible results it achieves. How wrong! This should not be the focus of my praying, otherwise it becomes an emergency convenience—something to which I am driven by need. Perhaps the real question is, am I fellowshiping with God for HIMSELF, or only for MYSELF?

MANY DO NOT LIKE THE HARVEST THEY ARE NOW REAPING, yet are not wholly convinced it is the result of their earlier sowing. We cannot ignore the fact that God has built into the fabric of this universe a natural law: we reap exactly what we sow. Alas, there is no crop failure here! When we sow to the flesh, we reap corruption; when we sow to the Spirit, we reap eternal values. Which means we had better do some serious thinking about sowing proper seed today.

OUR STORIES TODAY are from a collection gathered through the years. I regret that I cannot always find their source. Each incident is intended to awaken our heart to more careful sowing. I'm sure many of us would like to go back and undo some past sowing. It is too late! But we can look forward to more wisely finishing life's race. Today we can make a deliberate choice.

More Diligent
in Proper Sowing

THE NAME OF JOHN G. PATON stands out as one of the noblest among missionaries. Few men evidenced more heroism and sacrifice than did that kingly soldier of the cross. In reading his biography one finds on the first page the secret. It is the memory of the family altar: his father reading the old family Bible twice a day and all the children kneeling and praying together. Paton says that in that home his father's influence made him all he was, and molded his missionary life and work.

Indeed, some things are taught, but there are some things that can only be "caught," such as a father's devotion to God and to His Word, a gentle, quiet spirit in the hour of crisis, and a confidence in God that passes all understanding.

We must ask ourselves the question, Will we delight in reaping tomorrow, what we are sowing today?

I know of two men who occasionally visited their father and mother at the old home place. In time the parents both went to their heavenly reward, and the sons needed to make some plans for the old home. One of them said to his brother, "If you'll allow me, I'll tear down the old house and build a summer home, and let you use it whenever you want to."

Accordingly, they took a trip out to the old homestead, back to the very spot which held so many sacred memories. When the two brothers, now past middle life and wealthy, arrived, they went into the house and looked around. One walked up and down in front of the old fireplace, and the other sat down.

Finally one said to the other. "You know, Bob, what I'm thinking about? I've changed my mind since I've been here. We're not going to tear down this old house. No—it must stand; we'll not tear it down."

"That is a strange thing," the other brother said, "because while I was walking up and down in front of the old fireplace, that is the same thing I was thinking about." He pointed to the chair in which his father used to sit. "Here is the old chair that father sat in when he read the Bible, when we had family worship, the chair around which we knelt as father lifted our hearts to God."

They stayed there two hours to talk things over. Both brothers got down on their knees by the old chair, repented and wept their hearts out before God. They both went back changed men, and from that day gave generously of their money and lived for God.

REAPING TIME HAD COME! In each of the above families we see parents who had been sowing—sowing indelible pictures in remembrance chambers, sowing attitudes, habits and values into young lives. No doubt each parent had claimed God's promise, "They that sow in tears shall reap in joy. He that goeth forth and weepeth, bearing precious seed, shall doubtless come again with rejoicing, bringing his sheaves with him" (Ps.126:5-6). Yes, God is a sure Rewarder!

If we sow a life of indifference to God, or profane or even careless language; if we fail to ask God's blessing at the table; if we think little or nothing of God's Word and expect our children to grow up and be spiritually mature, we and they, will only reap what we have sown.

IN GUIDEPOSTS MAGAZINE, Elda Mills tells us of her parent's faithful sowing during her girlhood days:

When I was a very young girl growing up in South Dakota, it often annoyed me that my parents put themselves out so much for total strangers. Our farm was on a windswept prairie, miles from the next farm, more miles from town—miles of unpaved road. Cars were always breaking down, bringing stranded strangers to our door day and night.

Those were depression days, hard times, when our farm wasn't always able to provide enough food for our large family. Even so, my parents were always ready to share. Whenever I complained that their hospitality was depriving the family of our own needs, either my father or my mother had a Bible passage as an answer. That was hard to argue against, no matter how often I tried.

I remember the stormy night when a knock came at the door and there in the dim light of our kerosene lamp stood a drenched, barefooted man. His car was stuck in mud; in it were four women, he said, and one was ill. Out went Dad and my brother with a team of horses to bring the strangers back. Not only did my mother give up her room so that the women could have a place to sleep—two on a bed, two on the floor—but mother herself slept in a rocking chair in my room.

She was up early to fix a huge breakfast for our unexpected guests. When I grumbled that she was feeding the strangers better than she would have fed the family, she just said, "Matthew twenty-five, forty."

I looked it up. "Inasmch as ye have done it unto one of the least of these My brethren, ye have done it unto Me." So I tried to swallow my resentment.

That was just one episode. Another morning I awoke to find an old gray-haired man with a grizzled beard in our kitchen, hunched over a bowl of oatmeal. When Dad fried some eggs for the guest and for himself, the old man raked all four eggs onto his own plate and began to eat. Dad never battered an eye, even though that meant there would be no eggs for him that morning, or until our hens laid again. When Dad saw the look of irritation on my face, he said softly: "John twenty-one, sixteen."

I looked it up. "He said unto him, Feed My sheep." All right! But feed them everything?

Then there was the cold spring day when a shivering man walked past our house in his shirt sleeves, and my father took off his coat and gave it to him. Later, when Dad went out to do his chores, he put on his other coat, the one with the patch on the sleeves. Again I must have had that angry look on my face, and this time Dad simply said, "Luke three, eleven."

I looked it up. "He that hath two coats, let him impart to him that hath none." All right? But give away your best coat?

One windy summer day a family stopped at our house because of car trouble. My mother offered them a plate of hot ears of corn we were supposed to have ourselves and loaves of the fresh bread she had just baked. They ate away, while my brother worked on their car. I was too young to appreciate the attention of their teenage son, who teased me and tugged at my braids. I was glad when they finally drove off.

Before I could complain, my mother said, "Ecclesiastes eleven, one."

I looked it up. "Cast thy bread upon the waters: for thou shalt find it after many days." I was hoping that didn't mean those people would come back.

Today that is my favorite verse. Here's why: Over the years, my parents corresponded with that family. When they were passing by, they'd stop and visit for a spell. The son continued to tease me and tug at my braids until I outgew them.

But I never outgrew the boy. Today that *boy* is the man who is my husband![1]

From this lovely testimony we uncover three important insights. In Elda's parents we admire the character qualities which they were sowing in their children. (1) Since they were rich in God's Word, they implanted It in their children. (2) Having developed a gentle, quiet spirit, they could model gentleness and quietness to their offspring. (3) Since they had liberality of heart, they planted the seeds of generosity in their children. May God be praised that we can do likewise.

(1) SOWING GOD'S WORD. Through many years of observation, I have become increasingly aware that the best way to walk in much practical wisdom is to be rich in God's Word. Paul exhorts us, "Let the word of Christ dwell in you richly in all wisdom; teaching and admonishing one another in psalms and hymns and spiritual songs, singing with grace in your hearts to the Lord" (Col.3:16).

Alas, there are thousands who expect to reap God's blessings without proper sowing. Have you ever heard someone complain that prayer just didn't work for them "I prayed, and prayed—but nothing happened. God failed me!" Of course most folk would never express such an attitude so blatantly, yet hidden deep in the heart of many of God's children lurks this frustration, "Prayer may work for others, but it doesn't work for me."

In his book, FREEDOM TO GROW, Ernie Gruen answers folk who talk like this. He says, "God always works on the basis of principles, not on the basis of magic. If you don't understand this, you are going to be confused."[2]

He continues, "Do you have enough faith to believe that if you went out to the back yard and prayed over the ground, without plowing and without planting—saying, 'in the name of Jesus I ask for a beautiful, bountiful garden,' that suddenly a row of carrots would pop up, and then a row of beans and a row of corn? I know that all things are possible with God, but do you have such faith to believe for a garden without planting a garden?"

"You know it won't happen that way. And yet, in the spiritual realm, people very often expect that type of instant harvest ... they think they can plant just one seed a week, and pray when they get into trouble. Or they might decide to read the Bible twice a month, and then they look to their spiritual garden and announce, 'God, You failed me! Where are the results? Where are the vegetables? I prayed and You didn't come through! How can I trust You and Your promises ... it just didn't work for me.' "(2)

There are some parents who never sow Bible principles into the lives of their children. It is true they attempt to force them to church, or impose their personal standards and convictions. Children may conform to some demands for a while, yet it will be temporary. It is like outwardly "wearing a suit of clothes" without having any inward reality. Such parents should not be surprised when their children challenge their authority. Until the Holy Spirit has worked reality into their hearts, such children will be rebellious, deceitful and unteachable. What I am trying to say is:

there is a "kind of" parental sowing
that produces REACTION to authority;
there is a parental modeling (sowing) of reality
that brings a RESPONSE to God.

Gruen continues to exhort parents: "As parents you can't just do your own thing, follow your own will, and then push a God-button and plead, 'Okay, God, please cause my children to be holy.' God replies when He hears that—if you are really listening—'Can't you see that you have been violating principles in my Book? You're setting a poor example for them ... developing wrong attitudes ... then you dare to think that by praying and praying your family will turn out ... without any proper sowing.' And isn't it strange that such folk will announce, 'Well, I don't know. I prayed for my kids. I don't know what happened. God didn't answer my prayer.' "

On occasion, God may hear and intervene in answering some desperate plea for help, but it is unthinkable that God should ignore the very laws He has established: you reap what you sow. "Do not be deceived, God is not mocked" (Gal.6:7). Don't try to make God look ridiculous by trying to outwit Him. Don't be led astray. You cannot violate the principles of God without suffering consequences; neither can you put these principles into practice in

God's way without harvesting a crop, pleasing and abundant, from the generous hand of God.

(2) SOW A GENTLE, QUIET SPIRIT: Many perhaps never quite grasp the fact that what we are in our spirit, we are continually sowing. If we are hostile, we sow that; if we are brash, we sow that; if we are peaceful, we sow that; if gentle, grateful, generous, gracious, we sow that. "As in water face answereth to face, so the heart of man to man" (Prov.27:19). It should be remembered that while some things are taught, many vital things are caught.

Five young men left their homes in Pennsylvania for the great Northwest. One returned later seemingly much stronger because of the experience through which he had passed. When asked the reason why he had not taken the downward way of the other four, he replied, "Because I carried with me a picture of my home. I remember the last morning the family was together. We all sat down to breakfast as usual. Father was at one end of the table and my precious mother at the other. Realizing that there was to be a breaking of home ties within a few hours, conversation was not very brisk that morning.

"After breakfast, as was my father's custom, he took the old family Bible and started to read the morning lesson. But he didn't get very far. A lump kept coming up in his throat, and he was so blinded by tears that he could not read. After mother finally finished the chapter, we knelt to pray. Father started his prayer, but he hadn't gotten very far until that same lump came up in his throat and choked back further expression. Then mother reached over and put her hand on my shoulder and began to pray. It was the vision of that last morning in the atmosphere of my godly home, and the remembrance of my precious mother's prayer that steered me right. I could not bear the thought of breaking the heart of my mother and father, and of dishonoring my Lord and Savior whom they taught me to love."

Some day, and it may be we'll have to wait until God opens the books in eternity, we'll discover how often a meek, gentle and quiet spirit was being sown in lives, and we have been quite unaware until the time for reaping.

(3) SOWING GENEROSITY: We take another look at the parents of Elda Mills, and ponder whether they had any awareness of the diligent planting in the heart of their daughter. Indeed it is blessed when a daughter can look back with thanksgiving to God for the planting of His Word, of a gentle spirit and of generosity.

If you will allow me this moment for thanksgiving, I guess I can identify with Elda Mills and her family because I also experienced those very difficult depression years in South Dakota. And in similar manner my parents also held open-house for scores who passed through our small village. I now realize that God planted many choice memories of a home with parents who always honored God. Surely it is true that no "bread cast upon the waters—when given unto Him—will ever be lost." In His own time, God has a way of sending it back.

QUICKENING FROM GOD'S WORD. . . read 2 Cor.9:6-15 (Phillips).

Please note that our sowing is not merely for what we can reap, but that God might have His harvest of thanksgiving:

All I will say is that poor sowing means a poor harvest, and generous sowing means a generous harvest.
Let everyone give as his heart tells him, neither grudgingly nor under compulsion, for God loves the man whose heart is in his gift. After all, God can give you everything that you need, so that you may always have sufficient both for yourselves and for giving away to other people. As the Scripture says:
He scattered abroad, he hath given to the poor,
His righteousness abideth for ever.
He who gives the seed to the sower and turns that seed into bread to eat, will give you the seed of generosity to sow and, for harvest, the satisfying bread of good deeds done. The more you are enriched by God, the more scope will there be for generous giving, and your gifts, administered through us, will mean that many will thank God. For your giving does not end in meeting the wants of your fellow-Christians. IT ALSO RESULTS IN AN OVERFLOWING TIDE OF THANKSGIVING TO GOD.
Moreover, your very giving proves the reality of your faith, and that means that men thank God that you practice the gospel that you profess to believe in, as well as for the actual gifts you make to them and to others. And yet further, men will pray for you and feel drawn to you because you have obviously received a generous measure of the grace of God.
Thank God, then, for His indescribable generosity to you!

<u>AWAKEN MY HEART</u>. . . to more diligent sowing.

Father, I want to know the way of a soft answer. Then I can know how to pour soothing oil in the wounds of so many who are hurting.

I do thank You for parents who took time to carefully plant seed in our fertile hearts when we were young. I see how they modeled a right spirit in moments of stress, and generously shared from their sometimes limited supply. Yes, Lord, You have been so faithful in providing for them throughout these 86 years. You are wholly trustworthy, and my heart is quite awakened to sing with . . .

<u>OVERFLOWING GRATITUDE.</u>

Great is Thy faithfulness! O God my Father,
   There is no shadow of turning with Thee;
Thou changest not, Thy compassions they fail not;
   As Thou hast been Thou forever wilt be.
      Great is Thy faithfulness!
      Great is Thy faithfulness!
      Morning by morning new mercies I see;
      All I have needed Thy hand hath provided—
      Great is Thy faithfulness, Lord, unto me!

Summer and winter, and springtime and harvest,
   Sun, moon and stars in their courses above,
Join with all nature in manifold witness
   To Thy great faithfulness, mercy and love.
         (William M. Runyan)

PRAYER REQUESTS   DATE ANSWERED

_____
_____
_____
_____
_____
_____
_____
_____
_____
_____
_____
_____
_____
_____
_____
_____
_____
_____
_____
_____

INSIGHTS FROM LESSON

_____
_____
_____
_____
_____
_____
_____
_____
_____
_____
_____
_____
_____
_____
_____
_____
_____
_____
_____

DAY THIRTEEN

THE DISCIPLINE OF KEEPING a fixed time for meeting the Lord each day will be severely tested. You have already discovered that—haven't you? The temptation to quit, or to miss a day will ever be with you. Remember, you may lose one battle, but you need not lose the war—if you maintain complete honesty in your fellowship. If some emergency hinders you, continue the next day with the confidence that only one day was lost—you have the whole life-race yet before you.

IN THIS LESSON . . . we uncover another most critical issue: What to do when things are "locked tight" in our home or church? We must get behind the outward problem. We must see how preaching and praying are often a futile exercise, because the Enemy has become entrenched in strong-hold positions and needs to be challenged and routed.

This is not a work for the faint-hearted! Since God has already won the victory, we who go forth in His name do take the initiative when we proclaim the victorious message that Jesus has been resurrected and enthroned. Once again we can appreciate our partnership with God, and realize why we need to better understand God's ways.

OUR STORY told by Watchman Nee is from his book, SIT, WALK, STAND. We encourage you to further study this book which deals with the important aspect of victory, as seen in the epistle to the Ephesians.

Standing in His Victory

WATCHMAN NEE relates how he went with a team of seven to an island off the coast of China for a preaching mission from Jan.1st to the 15th:

Though we labored systematically and hard, and though we found the people of the village courteous, we had little fruit . . . and we began to wonder why this was.

On Jan.9th we were outside preaching. Brother Wu with some others was in one part of the village and suddenly asked publicly: "Why will none of you believe?" Someone in the crowd replied at once: "We have a god—one god—Ta Wang, and he has never failed us. He is an effective god."

"How do you know that you can trust him?" asked Wu. "We have held his festival procession every January for 286 years. The chosen day is revealed by divination beforehand, and every year without fail his day is a perfect one without rain or cloud," was the reply.

"When is the procession this year?" "It is fixed for January 11th at eight in the morning." "Then," said brother Wu impetuously, "I promise you that it will certainly rain on the 11th." At once there was an outburst of cries from the crowd: "That is enough! We don't want to hear any more preaching. If there is rain on the 11th, then your God is God!"

I was elsewhere in the village when this occurred. As soon as I heard of it, I saw that it was most serious. The news had spread like wildfire, and before long, over twenty thousand people would know about it.

137

What were we to do? We stopped our preaching at once, and gave ourselves to prayer. We asked the Lord to forgive us if we had overstepped ourselves. I tell you, we were in deadly earnest. What had we done? Had we made a terrible mistake, or dare we ask God for a miracle?

The more you want an answer to prayer from God, the more you desire to be clear with Him. There must be no doubt about fellowship—no shadow between . . . . We did not mind being thrown out if we had done something wrong. After all, you can't drag God into a thing against His will! But, we reflected, this would mean an end to the Gospel testimony in the island, and Ta-wang would reign supreme for ever. What should we do? Should we leave now?

Up to this point we had feared to pray for rain. Then, like a flash, there came the word to me: "Where is the God of Elijah?" It came with such clarity and power that I knew it was from God. Confidently I announced to the brothers, "I have the answer. The Lord will send rain on the 11th." Together we thanked Him, and then, full of praise, we went out—all seven of us—and told everyone. We could accept the devil's challenge in the name of the Lord, and we would broadcast our acceptance.

That evening the herbalist made two very pointed observations. Undoubtedly, he said, Ta-wang was an effective god. The devil was with that image. Their faith in him was not groundless. Alternatively, if you preferred a rationalistic explanation, here was a whole village of fishermen. For two or three months on end the men were at sea, and on the 15th they would be out again. They, of all people, should know by long experience when it would not rain for two or three days ahead.

This disturbed us. As we went to our evening prayer, we all began once more to pray for rain—now! Then it was that there came to us a stern rebuke from the Lord. "Where is the God of Elijah?" Were we going to fight our way through this battle, or were we going to rest in the finished victory of Christ?

What had Elisha done when he spoke those words? He had laid claim in his own personal experience to the very miracle that his lord Elijah, now in the glory, had himself performed. In New Testament terms, he had taken his stand by faith on the ground of the finished work.

We confessed our sins again. "Lord," we said, "We don't need rain until the 11th morning." We went to bed, and next morning (the 10th) we set off for a neighboring island for a day's preaching. The Lord was very gracious, and that day three families turned to

Him, confessing Him publicly and burning their idols. We returned late, tired out but rejoicing. We could afford to sleep late tomorrow.

I was awakened by the direct rays of the sun through the single window of our attic. "This isn't rain!" I said. It was already past seven o'clock. I got up, knelt down and prayed. "Lord," I said, "please send the rain!" But once again, ringing in my ears came the word: "Where is the God of Elijah?" Humbled, I walked downstairs before God in silence. We sat down to breakfast—eight of us together, including our host—all very quiet. There was no cloud in the sky. But we knew God was committed. As we bowed to say grace before the food, I said, "I think the time is up. Rain must come now. We can bring it to the Lord's remembrance." Quietly we did so, and this time the answer came with no hint whatever of rebuke in it.

Even before our amen, we heard a few drops on the tiles. There was a steady shower as we ate our rice and were served with a second bowl. "Let us give thanks again," I said, and now we asked God for heavier rain. As we began on that second bowl of rice the rain was coming down in buckets-full. By the time we had finished, the street outside was already deep in water and the three steps at the door of the house were covered.

Soon we heard what had happened in the village. Already, at the first drop of rain, a few of the younger generation had begun to say openly, "There is God; there is no more Ta-wang! He is kept in by the rain."

But he wasn't. They carried him out on a sedan chair. Surely he would stop the shower! Then came the downpour. After only some ten or twelve yards, three of the coolies stumbled and fell. Down went the chair and Ta-wang with it, fracturing his jaw and his left arm.

Still determined, they carried out emergency repairs and put him back in the chair. Somehow, slipping and stumbling, they dragged or carried him half-way round the village. Then the floods defeated them. Some of the village elders, old men of 60 to 80 years, bareheaded and without umbrellas as their faith in Ta-wang's weather required, had fallen and were in serious difficulties. The procession was stopped and the idol taken into a house. Divination was made. "Today was the wrong day," came the answer. The festival is to be on the 14th with the procession at six in the evening."

Immediately as we heard this there came assurance in our hearts: "God will send rain on the 14th." We went to prayer. "Lord,

send rain on the 14th at 6:00 p.m. and give us four good days until then." That afternoon the sky cleared, and now we had a good hearing for the Gospel. The Lord gave us over thirty converts—real ones—in the village and in the island during those three short days.

The 14th broke, another perfect day, and we had good meetings. As the evening approached we met, and again, at the appointed hour, we quietly brought the matter to the Lord's remembrance. Not a minute late, His answer came with torrential rain and floods as before.

The next day our time was up, and we had to leave. We have not been back. Other workers asked for those islands and we never question anyone's claim to a field. But for us the essential point was that Satan's power in that idol had been broken, and that is an eternal thing. Ta-wang was no more an "effective god". The salvation of souls would follow, but was in itself secondary to this vital and unchanging fact.[1]

WHY THIS AMAZING VICTORY?

If you are to become partners with God in His ways, you must understand spiritual warfare. Perhaps in your own life or ministry you have encountered a "locked-up" situation, as did this team of seven on the island. When things are locked up tight, whether in a home, church, community or nation, it is usually because the Enemy of God has become entrenched. For years, through deception, he has established strong-hold positions which will come down only as we boldly challenge in the name of the Lord Jesus.

GOD HAS ALREADY WON! When our Lord Jesus rose from the grave as Victor and then ascended to the right hand of God where He is now seated, once and for all the Enemy was exposed as the defeated one. Because of His enthronement, we can now move as militant ones who take the initiative in declaring the good news of His victory. Since the battle was won at Calvary and demonstrated in His resurrection,

we do not fight FOR A PLACE, but

FROM A PLACE of victory!

Thus we are told to "stand against . . . to withstand . . . and to stand" (Eph.6:12-14).

UNDERSTAND THREE THINGS

First, we must recognize that the battle ground is in the "high places". Let me explain. In each individual the human spirit is that "high place" which must be wholly yielded to God. Likewise, in our homes, in our church, in our nation, there are high places of rebellion, unteachableness, etc. which must be dealt with before God's total victory can be realized. Those who are placed in positions of authority— whether a husband, or a father in the home, the pastor or elders in a church, or the rulers in local government— each must be in submission to God, or there will be unyielded high places standing in resistance. These are strong-holds from which the enemy has ground to work.

To illustrate: A missionary visiting a girl's boarding school in Cuba asked, "May I tell the girls something after dinner?" The director replied, "They still have to do all their homework for tomorrow. You may speak to them for only five minutes, no more!" Here was a woman with a dominion spirit who had only one concern—fulfilling policy. While her intentions seemed good, she actually had little interest in the spiritual welfare of the children, and was not sensitive to God.

As the missionary spoke—it happened! After four minutes the lights suddenly went out. The children clamored, "Please will you continue until the lights go on again? We cannot work in the dark!" So the missionary told all sorts of adventures, journeys and meetings with other children around the world, and was then able to share about the Lord Jesus—who He was, and what He wanted in each one of their lives.

After an hour the lights came on again. The children started their home-work. A little girl came to the missionary, putting her arms around her neck, and whispered: "I believe that Jesus broke the lights so that you could tell us about Him." Well, we can rejoice that the missionary's spirit was submitted to the Lord, to be available for Him to use, and He made a way for the message by overruling a strong spirit. His government prevailed!

Second, we must have a special "prophetic word" for each occasion. Consider! Until Watchman Nee received a special "rhema", they were in doubt and bewilderment. Then it came! "Where is the God of Elijah?" Like a fresh breeze to their sagging spirits, God was saying , "What I did for Elijah in his crisis hour I will do for you."

This is not so unusual. Down through the centuries many of God's servants have "gotten a verse", which was quickened to them in their moment of need. For them it meant personal assurance that God was working for them as they stood for His full purposes.

It was so when King Jehoshaphat was surrounded by enemy nations. In desperation Israel fasted and prayed; then a prophetic word came through Jehaziel:

"Be not afraid . . . the battle is not yours but God's.
. . . set yourselves, stand ye still, and see the salvation . . ."
(2 Chron.20:15,17).

We know how mightily God performed in their behalf as they obeyed the special Word given to them. Please note this difference: Jehoshaphat and the people could stand on God's *general* Word (logos) which had already been given, but when they received His *special* Word (rhema) through the prophet, they moved in new confidence.

"Believe in the Lord . . . so shall ye be *established*; believe His prophets, so shall ye *prosper*" (vs.20).

How thankful we are for every page of God's Word; how grateful we are when He quickens a special portion to meet our immediate need.

Third, there is a *time to pray*, but also a *time to boldly stand* in God's victory. When enemy kingdoms resist God's work, it is time to speak the word of authority in faith. When the Watchman Nee team announced there would be no rain on those days, they were standing with God. We must remember that though it might appear every battle is down here, yet there is warfare raging in the heavenlies. God could smash these resistant powers and principalities by Himself. Yet He has chosen to do it through men. Someone has rightly said,

"Without God man cannot;
without man God will not."

This is God's self-limiting way to bring man into cooperation with Himself.

When that taunting giant, Goliath, mockingly defied the army of the living God, and invited a man to come against him, young David—whom God had been preparing for that hour—accepted the challenge. There he stood in faith, utterly dependent upon God as His Shield, refusing to accept the armour of man, and daring to speak forth this word of faith:

"Thou comest to me with a sword, and with a spear, and with a shield; but I come to you in the name of the Lord of hosts, the God of the armies of Israel, whom you have defied. This day will the Lord deliver you into my hand" (1 Sam.17).

And He did!

It becomes clear to us that the real battle in the heavenlies had its counterpart in the struggle between David and Goliath. There is a time to pray; but this was the time for David to go forth in the name of the Lord. Also notice that David was moving in a realm of authority granted to him by king Saul.

We have seen how (1) every high places must be wholly yielded to God. Because David and Jehoshaphat were rightly alligned with God's government, He gave victory. We have seen how (2) a "prophetic word" encouraged both Jehoshaphat and the team to stand with God and watch Him work. We have seen (3) in each instance that a "faith declaration" was required. Prayer had its place, but taking strongholds required the bold action of speaking in faith. Thank God, we too can move mountains in our day as we learn to follow these principles.

A word of caution. In each instance we see how the "faith declaration" appeared as foolishnes in the eyes of men. When the team announced it would rain, the fishermen scoffed; when youthful David announced he was moving out against Goliath, they laughed; when the choir appointed by Jehoshaphat stood in full view on the cliff in front of the army, it seemed like utter foolishness. But "God's foolishness is wiser than man's wisdom."

Every David will understand what it means to "go it alone." Only God knows what He has spoken to David's heart. To everyone else it will seem foolish. Any man who moves without hearing from God, will demonstrate the foolishness of man. And because we have many who would imitate David or Johoshaphat—we have much *foolishness of man*, and little *foolishness of God*.

WHEN VICTORY DOESN'T COME

Perhaps you are one of God's children who questions why this kind of victory does not seem to work in your own experience. You have repeatedly tried and failed. May I suggest that there are three possible reasons why many do not stand victorious in their conflict:

(1) The "spirit of the world" prevails in their life. (1 Cor.2:12) There is no warfare for them because they are fundamentally compatible with the Enemy, not at enmity with him.

(2) Others may be at "ease in Zion," a condition against which God pronounces a woe (Amos 6:1). While they might insist they enjoy the "rest of the Lord," they have actually defected from the battle. This becomes evident, for they are not vexed by the religious error and moral corruption around them. Like Moab of old, they have simply settled on their "lees" (Jer.48:10-13), and are

complacent and comfortable when they should be burdened and distressed—concerned enough to move with God to enforce His victory in lives.

(3) Finally, there must be a constant faith-expectancy and watchfulness. Many become weary in the fight, and abandon the field to the Enemy because they do not see visible success immediately. No, we are called to be diligent in trusting, to be watchful, to walk circumspectly, above all—to keep our eyes continually upon Him. We do not realize how much God is working on behalf of His children. Someday we shall understand just how much victory He enforces when we "stand!" with Him.

A troop of rebels in the Congo came into a villlage. The leader asked "What is that house?" "That is the house of God." He took a stone to throw into it, but at that same moment he was killed by a bullet. The bullet must have been misfired by one of his own people. In another village rebels gathered in a hut to discuss their devilish plan of killing all the Christians. At that very moment lightning struck the hut and all the rebels were killed.

When other rebels advanced on a school where two hundred children of missionaries lived, they planned to kill both children and teachers. Those in the school heard of their danger and went to prayer. Their only protection was a fence and a couple of soldiers; while the enemy, who came closer and closer, amounted to several hundred. When the rebels were close by, suddenly something happened. They turned around and fled! The next day the same thing happened and again on the third day. When one of the rebels was wounded, the doctor dressing his wounds asked him: "Why did you not break into the school as you planned?"

He responded, "We could not do it. We saw hundreds of soldiers in white uniforms and we became scared." In Africa soldiers never wear white uniforms; it must have been angels! What an amazing thing, that the Lord should open the eyes of the enemy to see Gods protective angels standing on duty.

QUICKENING FROM GOD'S WORD

The prophet Isaiah gives us these encouraging words:
"Yes, truth is gone, and anyone who tries a better life is soon attacked. The Lord saw all the evil and was displeased to find no steps taken against sin. He saw no one was helping you, and won-

dered that no one intervened. Therefore He Himself stepped in to save you through his mighty power and justice. He put on righteousness as armor, and the helmet of salvation on His head. He clothed Himself with robes of vengeance and of godly fury" (Isa.59:15-18 L.B.).

"So shall they fear the name of the Lord from the west, and his glory from the rising of the sun. When the Enemy shall come in like a flood, the Spirit of the Lord shall lift up a standard against him." (Vs.19 K.J.).

THE GREATEST NEED OF THIS HOUR is for men to draw the battle lines clearly. There is so much mixture, so much double-mindedness, so much compromise. Who is really on the Lord's side? Who will stand with Him even though it means persecution and deprivation? Hallelujah! By Thy grace we shall!

We are greatly encouraged, for we see God raising up an army of intercessors who know their privilege of standing with God to fully enforce His victory. Will you be one who has heard His call to this partnership? However dark and impossible things may look, we are sure that God will have a Glorius Church standing with Him announcing the triumphancy of our Lord Jesus.

AWAKEN MY HEART... to participate in this calling.

Father, I confess that too often I have been stopped cold— made utterly ineffective—because I did not recognize the entrenched foe. There have been locked-up situations that I could have released. I now understand why praying was not enough. It is evident that mountains do not move by praying alone, but by "saying" to them— BE MOVED! in the name of the Lord.

What a difference it makes when I can view from the heavenlies how You set the Enemy in disarray. What good news I can announce—You have already won! The final outworking of all Your glorious triumph only awaits my cooperation.

Yes, it is with new confidence that I can now expect You to expose those "locked-up high places" and I can claim triumph in my own life, in my home, in my work, in my church and in my community. Help me to recognize when I am about to stoop to flesh and blood warfare, as I have done in the past. Help me to "stand with You" in the battle, neither forcing the initiative on my own, nor passively waiting, as though assuming You had something yet to do.

OVERFLOWING GRATITUDE

My heart is tuned to the militant sounds of Your marching army. (Tune—Onward Christian soldiers)

At the name of Jesus, Satan's host doth flee,
On then Christian soldiers, on to victory!
Hell's foundations quiver at the shout of praise.
Brothers, lift your voices, loud your anthems raise.
    Onward, Christian soldiers, marching as to war,
    With the Cross of Jesus going on before.

Onward, then, ye people! join our happy throng;
Blend with ours your voices in the triumph song.
Glory, laud and honor unto Christ, the King;
This thro' countless ages men and angels sing.
                  (S.Baring-Gould)

PRAYER REQUESTS   DATE ANSWERED

_____

_____

_____

_____

_____

_____

_____

_____

_____

_____

INSIGHTS FROM LESSON

_____

_____

_____

_____

_____

_____

_____

_____

_____

_____

DAY FOURTEEN

MANY WHO HAVE BEEN ACCUSTOMED to a ten minute devotional at the breakfast table before rushing into the day's activities, have realized by now that it takes time to fellowship. Each lesson could have been much shorter, and that would have allowed more time for praying and meditating or writing down your insights. I trust you have taken time to do this.

Have you considered these words of an old hymn...

> TAKE TIME to be holy,
>   Speak oft with Thy Lord.
> Spend much time in secret
>   With Jesus alone—

Yes, to fellowship takes time! Have you noticed how you always make time for some things you consider most important? In a love relationship with Him there will be much waiting...listening...pondering...as He awakens your heart to a fuller seeing His purposes and ways.

TODAY WE READ about a young soldier whose love for the Lord Jesus goes far beyond what we might call normal love—I have chosen to call it EXTRAVAGANT LOVE. We see how God can woo even a very young man to such a single-hearted communion with Himself that nothing else matters in life but pleasing Him.

IN READING THIS STORY your heart will be enlarged and stretched toward the Lord. And most likely certain questions will develop which He alone can answer—and that is the way it ought to be.

Extravagant Love Exposes

THIS TRUE ACCOUNT, taken from an old, out of print book, is the personal testimony of a Jewish doctor:[1]

I was a surgeon in the United States Army during the Civil War. After the battle of Gettysburg, there were hundreds of wounded soldiers in my hospital. Many were wounded so severely that a leg or an arm, or sometimes both, needed to be amputated.

One of these was a boy who had only been in the service for three months. Since he was too young to be a soldier, he had enlisted as a drummer. When my assistants came to give him chloroform before the amputation, he turned his head and refused it. When they told him that it was doctor's orders, he said, "Please send the doctor to me."

I came to his bedside and said, "Young man, why do you refuse chloroform? When I found you on the battlefield, you were so far gone that I almost didn't bother to pick you up. But when you opened those large blue eyes, it occurred to me that you had a mother somewhere who might be thinking of you at that very moment. I didn't want you to die on the field, so I had you brought here. You've lost so much blood that you're just too weak to live through an operation without chloroform. You'd better let me give you some."

He laid his hand on mine, looked me in the face and said, "Doctor, one Sunday afternoon, when I was nine years old, I gave my heart to Christ. I learned to trust Him then, and I've been trusting Him ever since. I know I can trust Him now. He is my

149

strength. He will support me while you amputate my arm and leg."
I asked him if he would at least let me give him a little brandy.

Again he looked at me and said, "Doctor, when I was five years old, my mother knelt by my side with her arms around me, and said, 'Charlie, I am praying to Jesus that you will never take even one drink of alcohol. Your father died a drunkard, and I've asked God to use you to warn people against the dangers of drinking, and to encourage them to love and serve the Lord.' I am now seventeen years old, and I have never had anything stronger than tea or coffee. There is a very good chance that I am about to die and to go into the presence of my God. Would you send me there with brandy on my breath?"

I will never forget the look that boy gave me. At that time I hated Jesus, but I respected that boy's loyalty to his Saviour. And when I saw how he loved and trusted Him to the very end, something deeply touched my heart. I did for that boy what I had never done for any other soldier—I asked him if he wanted to see his chaplain.

Chaplain R. knew the boy well from having seen him frequently at the tent prayer meetings. Taking his hand, he said, "Charlie, I'm sorry to see you like this." "Oh, I'm all right, sir," Charlie answered. "The doctor offered me chloroform, but I told him I didn't want any. Then he wanted to give me some brandy, which I didn't want either. So now, if my Saviour calls me, I can go to Him in my right mind."

"You might not die, Charlie," said the chaplain, "but if the Lord does call you home, is there anything I can do for you after you're gone?"

"Chaplain, please reach under my pillow and take my little Bible. My mother's address is inside. Please send it to her, and write a letter for me. Tell her that since I left home, I have never let a single day pass—no matter if we were on the march, on the battlefield, or in the hospital—without reading a portion of God's Word, and daily praying that He would bless her."

"Is there anything else I can do for you, my lad?" asked the chaplain. "Yes—please write a letter to the Sunday school teacher of the Sands Street Church in Brooklyn, New York. Tell him that I've never forgotten his encouragement, good advice, and many prayers for me. They have helped me and comforted me through all the dangers of battle. And now, in my dying hour, I thank the Lord for my dear old teacher, and ask Him to bless and strengthen him. That is all."

Then turning to me, he said, "I'm ready, doctor. I promise I won't even groan while you take off my arm and leg, if you don't offer me chloroform." I promised, but I didn't have the courage to take the knife in my hand without first going into the next room and taking a little brandy myself.

While cutting through the flesh, Charlie Coulson never groaned. But when I took the saw to separate the bone, the lad took the corner of his pillow in his mouth, and all I could hear him whisper was, "O Jesus, blessed Jesus! Stand by me now." He kept his promise. He never groaned.

I couldn't sleep that night. Whichever way I tossed and turned, I saw those soft blue eyes, and when I closed my own eyes, the words, "Blessed Jesus, stand by me now," kept ringing in my ears. A little after midnight, I finally left my bed and visited the hospital—a thing I had never done before unless there was an emergency. I had such a strange and strong desire to see that boy. When I got there, an orderly told me that sixteen of the badly wounded soldiers had died. "Was Charlie Coulson one of them?" I asked. "No, sir," he answered, "he's sleeping as sweetly as a babe."

When I came to his bed, one of the nurses said that at about nine o'clock, two members of the Y.M.C.A. came through the hospital to read and sing a hymn. Chaplain R. was with them, and he knelt by Charlie's bed and offered up a fervent and soul-stirring prayer. Then, while still on their knees, they sang one of the sweetest of all hymns, "Jesus, Lover of My Soul." Charlie sang along with them, too. I couldn't understand how that boy, who was in such horrible pain, could sing.

Five days after I performed the operation, Charlie sent for me, and it was from him that I heard my first Gospel sermon. "Doctor," he said, "my time has come. I don't expect to see another sunrise. I want to thank you with all my heart for your kindness to me. I know you are Jewish, and that you don't believe in Jesus, but I want you to stay with me, and see me die trusting my Saviour to the last moment of my life."

I tried to stay, but I just couldn't. I didn't have the courage to stand by and see a Christian boy die rejoicing in the love of that Jesus whom I hated. So I hurriedly left the room.

About twenty minutes later an orderly came and found me sitting in my office with my hands covering my face. He told me that Charlie wanted to see me. "I've just seen him," I answered, "and I can't see him again." "But Doctor, he says he must see you once more before he dies." So I made up my mind to go and see

Charlie, say an endearing word, and let him die. However, I was determined that nothing he could say would influence me in the least bit, so far as his Jesus was concerned.

When I entered the hospital room I saw he was sinking fast, so I sat down by his bed. Asking me to take his hand, he said, "Doctor, I love you because you are a Jew. The best friend I have found in this world was a Jew." I asked him who that was, and he answered, "Jesus Christ, and I want to introduce you to Him before I die. Will you promise me, Doctor, that what I am about to say to you, you will never forget?"

I promised, and he said, "Five days ago, while you amputated my arm and leg, I prayed to the Lord Jesus Christ and asked Him to make His love known to you."

Those words went deep into my heart. I couldn't understand how, when I was causing him the most intense pain, he could forget all about himself and think of nothing but his Saviour and my unconverted soul. All I could say to him was, "Well, my dear boy, you will soon be all right." With these words I left him, and twelve minutes later he fell asleep, "safe in the arms of Jesus."

Hundreds of soldiers died in my hospital during the war, but I only followed one to the grave, and that was Charlie Coulson. I rode three miles to see him buried. I had him dressed in a new uniform, and placed in an officer's coffin, with a United States flag over it.

That boy's dying words made a deep impression upon me. I was rich at that time so far as money was concerned, but I would have given every penny I possessed if I could have felt towards Christ as Charlie did. But that feeling cannot be bought with money. Alas, I soon forgot all about my Christian soldier's little sermon, but I could not forget the boy himself. Looking back, I now know that I was under deep conviction of sin at that time. But for nearly ten years I fought against Christ with all the hatred I had until finally the dear boy's prayer was answered, and I surrendered my life to the love of Jesus.

About a year-and-a-half after my conversion, I went to a prayer meeting one evening in Brooklyn. It was one of those meetings where Christians testify about the loving kindness of God. After several had spoken, an elderly lady stood up and said, "Dear friends, this may be the last time I have a chance to publicly share how good the Lord has been to me. My doctor told me yesterday that my right lung is nearly gone, and my left lung is failing fast, so at the best I have only a short time to be with you. But what is left of me belongs to Jesus. It's a great joy to know that I shall soon meet my son with Jesus in heaven.

"Charlie was not only a soldier for his country, but also a soldier for Christ. He was wounded at the battle of Gettysburg and was cared for by a Jewish doctor who amputated his arm and leg. He died five days after the operation. The chaplain of the regiment wrote me a letter, and sent me my boy's Bible. I was told that in his dying hour, my Charlie sent for that Jewish doctor, and said to him, 'Doctor, before I die I wish to tell you that five days ago, while you amputated my arm and leg, I prayed to the Lord Jesus Christ for you.' "

As I heard this lady speak, I just couldn't sit still! I left my seat, ran across the room, and taking her hand said, "God bless you, my dear sister. Your boy's prayer has been answered! I am the Jewish doctor that Charlie prayed for, and his Saviour is now my Saviour! The love of Jesus has conquered my soul."

In reading this account our heart has been strangely warmed, but even more, it has been exposed! When we read about someone who expressed such unusual devotion, are we faced with our own coldness? Do we justify our lack of love? Does it force us to a new honesty?

In Charlie Coulson, along with his utter simplicity, we see four admirable qualities: assurance, rest, love and commitment. But we also see GOD'S FAITHFULNESS in responding to these four.

First, let us consider God's . . .

FAITHFULNESS IN DRAWING THE DOCTOR to Himself. We are not told how long this took, but once again we are encouraged that God does answer the prayers of those who mean business with Him. Charlie had asked God for his doctor's conversion. The unselfish devotion to Jesus that Jewish doctor saw in him could not be forgotten. Like Saul of Tarsus, who had seen the devotion of Stephen to his Lord as he was martyred, this doctor was on God's hook, just waiting to be pulled in. Next, let us consider . . .

GOD'S FAITHFULNESS IN DIRECTING THE STEPS of His children. While some may feel it was mere coincidence that the Jewish doctor and Charlie's mother met at the same prayer meeting on the same night, we know that neither of them attended that meeting with any understanding that they would meet each other, or share as they did.

It is important for us to recognize that some times God will direct our steps instead of giving us understanding. Often it is not expedient, nor is it wise for God to inform us what or how He is planning to work. In this instance, it seems the most convenient way was to direct the steps of the doctor and Charlie's mother to the same meeting. Yes, sometimes . . .

GOD DIRECTS OUR STEPS, sometimes HE GIVES UNDERSTANDING.

Since the Lord is DIRECTING our steps, why try to understand everything that happens . . .(Prov.20:24 L.B.).	I will instruct thee and teach thee in the way which thou shalt go . . . (Ps.32:8).
A man's heart deviseth his way; but the Lord directeth his steps (Prov.16:9).	I have given thee . . . an understanding heart; (1 Kings 3:12).
A wicked man hardeneth his face: as for the upright, He directh his way (Prov.21:29).	. . . in whom the Lord put wisdom and understanding to know how to work . . . (Ex.36:1).

What confidence this builds! Even during those times we were without understanding, God has been directing our steps and has brought us to a certain place in His proper timing. Thus we can see how all things can be directed to work for good, because we are the called according to His purpose.

It should not be assumed, however, that for us to seek understanding is wrong. On the contrary, while directing our steps may be good, for us to receive understanding is much better. Yes, through fellowship with God, we can share in His wisdom and understanding.

However, God never intended for this to be the normal way for us. God's Word says the horse and mule "have no understanding," but we know His children can enjoy such an intimate relationship with Him that a mere hint of His wishes will suffice to bring a response from them.

We share this, because too many of us have at times wished God would move us like puppets on a string, i.e. direct our feet with His "heavenly strings." It is true that at times God does seem to direct our steps, almost as if we were puppets moved by strings without our understanding; but that is not His normal order, nor should we seek for such, for that would disregard our high privilege of receiving more and more understanding through fellowship.

Now, we must see God's . . .

FAITHFULNESS IN RESPONDING TO CHARLIE'S CALL. In reading this incident many are quick to announce, "I could never endure such an ordeal. I do not have that kind of faith!" That is very true; none of us can boast of such.

You must not struggle for more faith, but learn the "rest of faith." Do not allow the Enemy to press you beyond your "measure of faith."

All through this painful ordeal we see how Charlie manifests a relaxed confidence. With him there is no struggle! He has moved beyond that initial faith given to us at salvation, to an increased proportion of faith which is developed in us through much testing. Charlie does expose us! Though a very young man, he has allowed God to take him through many lessons to a developed-faith, which is a fruit.(Gal.5:22)

Consider a critical point: Often young believers fall into much anguish because some zealous friend has been pressing them to trust beyond their "measure of faith". Anyone who is just beginning the faith-walk must not be expected to walk on the same level of faith as some more mature Christian who has already developed a greater "proportion of faith". I wish there were some shortcuts in developing faith. It seems we usually mature in our faith-walk only as we pass through fiery trials and tests.

Once we have experienced this increased proportion of faith (we have called the rest of faith) for ourselves, we will cease pressing others beyond their level of faith. Let no one imagine that he can go through such an ordeal as Charlie did, without first having an increased proportion of faith.

Don't whip yourself because of your lack; look to Him who will take you through each schoolroom lesson as fast as you are able. Thank God! There is ample grace for today; do not live in the expectation of what you might need tomorrow. Finally, we must see that . . .

EXTRAVAGANT LOVE IS NOT REQUIRED BUT IS RECEIVED.

Does God really require such love, as we see demonstrated in Charlie? Consider that moment when the doctor cuts the flesh and then saws the bone. Charlie calls out, "Blessed Jesus, stand by me now." It is in that most difficult moment I think I can hear my loving Father as He bends to whisper, "Charlie, I do see your trusting heart, and I do feel what you feel, and I do hear your call. I also see you demonstrating a love that goes far beyond what I would require."

Then there is a silence, while the bleeding heart of God pauses. "Charlie . . . while I do not require this, I do receive it. I receive the utter devotion you express to Me. I am grateful for what you are doing as an offering of thanksgiving to me for all that Jesus has done for you."

Then as I stoop closer to listen, I think I can hear Charlie responding, "Lord, this is my privilege, not a duty. When Jesus hung on the Cross, He could have taken the cup of vinegar, but He refused. You did not require that of Him, but You did most tenderly receive His supreme sacrifice."

Extravagant love! How else shall we explain such utter devotion? We would be most cautious in presenting this kind of love if we could not find it demonstrated in the Bible.

Do you remember when David and his men were hiding from king Saul in the caves of the wilderness? Some of David's mighty men overheard him wistfully long for a drink of water from the well at Bethlehem. Without hesitation three of those mighty men risked their lives, slipped through the enemy's lines and brought a drink to David. What a demonstration of love! How the heart of David was touched! It was not something David would ever require, but he did received it. In fact the drink of water was so precious to him that he poured it out as an offering before the Lord.

Watchman Nee explains,
David's mighty men need not have exposed themselves to danger in this way, but when they heard him express his longing, they hazarded their lives to satisfy it.

"The Christian should have a mind to suffer hardship. God will put a limit to our sufferings, but there should be no limit to our willingness to suffer for His testimony and for the salvation of men. This mind to suffer is not a sentimental idea; it is the verile spirit of those who disregard careful calculations and the crippling fear of going to extremes, all for love of Christ."

Only this morning as I was evaluating again whether to include this lesson, (some friends have felt it raises such difficult questions) I was led to open a book recently given to me by Judson Cornwall which I had not as yet read through. Strangely, as I opened some middle pages, my eyes fell upon these very words: "extravagant love." Dr. Cornwall is quoting from a mutual friend who says, "Worship is extreme submission and extravagant love . . . Daniel is an example of these two forces at work . . . . Even when the edict of the king made it life-threatening to do so, Daniel continued daily worship to God. His life was so surrendered to God that He refused to do things the king's way if it conflicted with God's revealed will. Yet his spirit remained loving toward God in the midst of all the pressure. Whether in training, in service, or in the lion's den, Daniel was a worshipper, for it was a way of life for him. His life was one of extreme submission to God and EXTRAVA-GANT LOVE poured out unto God."[3]

NOW I MUST TELL YOU ABOUT DAISY!

A few days ago I opened the diary of my dear friend, Daisy, the missionary who was riding in my car when we were struck by a drunken driver. In looking through her diary I found that Daisy had copied the following paragraph in it and then added this comment:

The young soldier, wounded in the Battle of the Bulge, listened as the Army surgeon spoke to him tenderly, "You're going to be all right, son. The only bad part is that you've lost a leg." "But," gasped the soldier, "I didn't lose it—I gave it!"

Daisy had written: "The best years of my life not are lost, but given to the Lord." (She had been imprisoned during World War II in a concentration camp.) "Given—not to an organization, not to a cause nor even to a mission field, but to HIM! Therefore it is all right if He is satisfied to put me aside. Perhaps He does want the remaining years, perhaps not, but can I not trust His wisdom and mercy?"

That diary entry was dated, April 13th, 1948.

It was just 23 days later, on Monday noon, May 6th, that Daisy was removed from my wrecked car. A few minutes later she left her broken body on the highway, and went to be with the One she had loved so very much.

While, in those early years, I had met soldiers of the Cross whose intense love exposed my own shallowness, nothing had so driven me to my knees as the EXTRAVAGANT LOVE expressed by Daisy.

In this lesson we have sought more to "open windows " than to bring you to conclusions. I'm sure there are many questions for which you need answers! Hold them before the Lord. There is much to ponder! The splendor of God's ways leaves us longing to know Him more and more.

Truly He is our Father who knows best when to withhold the understanding we beg for, and when to lovingly direct our steps. His Father-heart will never leave us struggling in faith, but ever woos us to a mature rest of faith. When we see extravagant love expressed, He is quick to remind us that such love is not REQUIRED, but is lovingly RECEIVED.

QUICKENING FROM GOD'S WORD. Read 1 Chron.11:10-25

These verses show us how much David's mighty men loved him. So much, that they put their lives in jeopardy just to satisfy his desire for water. If David, as mere leader among men should call forth such devotion from them, how much more should we demonstrate our love for the One who is Greater than David?

"David longed, and said, Oh that one would give me a drink of the water of the well of Bethlehem, that is at the gate! And three brake through the host of the Philistines, and drew water out of the well . . . and took it to David: but David would not drink of it, but poured it out to the Lord, and said, My God forbid it me, that I should do this thing: shall I drink the blood of these men that have put their lives in jeopardy? for with the jeopardy of their lives they brought it. These things did these three mightiest" (vs 17-19).

AWAKEN MY HEART

Father, I am sure there will be some as they read about Charlie, who will assume that You are against Your children using any medication during an operation, or at any time. Would You help them to really know You as a Father who understands our measure of faith and love. You only stir our comfortable nests, when we need to grow up and develop wings. Because You desire eagles who can soar in the higher levels, You will nudge us to the edge of our nest, and then push us out to help us develop our own wings of faith. Thank You, Father, for not pushing us out prematurely. You know exactly when we are ready to fly.

Forgive me, when I have been content to live according to minimum requirements. In a whole new way I can see extravagant love does not demand or require, yet when it is expressed—it is lovingly received.

Father, awaken my heart to realize that those who are "rich" can afford to be extravagant. That explains Your actions. Because You are rich in mercy and grace, You can be most extravagant in Your love toward us. I also can be extravagant! I can be rich— very rich in my appreciation of all You have done. Therefore I can be extravagant in my thanksgiving. As I become rich in my knowledge of Your ways, I can be extravagant in my praise. As I remember all the riches You have given me in Christ Jesus, I can be extravagant in my love. Yes, Father, I am continually discovering all my riches in Christ Jesus. That is why I want to be more extravagant in loving You.

OVERFLOWING GRATITUDE causes my heart to sing with the songwriter:

It passeth knowledge, that dear love of Thine,
My Saviour, Jesus; yet this soul of mine
Would of Thy love, in all its breadth and length,
Its height and depth, its everlasting strength,
    Know more and more.

It passeth telling, that dear love of Thine,
My Saviour, Jesus; yet these lips of mine
Would fain proclaim to sinners, far and near,
A love which can remove all guilty fear,
    And love beget.

It passeth praises, that dear love of Thine,
My Saviour, Jesus; yet this heart of mine
Would sing that love, so full, so rich so free,
Which brings a rebel sinner, such as me,
    Nigh unto God.

But though I cannot sing, or tell, or know
The fullness of Thy love, while here below,
My empty vessel I may freely bring;
O Thou, who art of love the living spring,
    My vessel fill.

Oh, fill me, Jesus, Saviour, with Thy love!
Lead, lead me to the living fount above;
Thither may I, in simple faith, draw nigh,
AND NEVER TO ANOTHER FOUNTAIN FLY,
    But UNTO THEE.

                              (M. Shekelton)

PRAYER REQUESTS   DATE ANSWERED

_____
_____
_____
_____
_____
_____
_____
_____
_____
_____
_____
_____
_____
_____
_____
_____
_____
_____
_____
_____
_____
_____
_____

INSIGHTS FROM LESSON

_____
_____
_____
_____
_____
_____
_____
_____
_____
_____
_____
_____
_____
_____
_____
_____

DAY FIFTEEN

TODAY WE FINISH OUR 15 DAY JOURNEY. Hopefully we have started some personal discipline; hopefully each of us will continue this time of daily fellowship with our Father until we finish our race. But we must be clear. Man's will-power can not sustain him in the discipline or rigor of the race. Knowing our own bankruptcy should have already taught us that God alone is our Source; and fellowship is the only means of receiving from that Source.

WHO CAN MEASURE ON THE SCALE of eternal values the worth of a man's work for God? Today we take a quick look at several whose lives manifest their dedication unto God. We ask, are there . . .

distinctive marks in those who LIVE UNTO FULLNESS?

We must banish the thought that God has some favorites or specialists who alone are destined to reach fullness. God forbid! I am convinced that none of us realizes how much our Father desires to accomplish in and through us. May God so awaken our hearts to that larger vision of what He has purposed for Himself, that we refuse to build kingdoms for ourselves, or become content in finding "some good thing" to do for God or man.

Living Unto Fullness

IT WAS EARLY MORNING. The visitor staying in the home of Dr. A.B. Simpson tiptoed quietly down the hall as he wished to slip out for a walk in the gray dawn.

As he passed the door of Dr. Simpson's study, the visitor glanced in. To his amazement he saw the old veteran seated at his desk, already dressed and busy at his work.

The visitor started to call out a greeting to Dr. Simpson, but noticed just in time that the elderly missionary statesman was reading his Bible and was deeply engrossed in his morning devotions. So the guest, still undetected, turned to leave.

Then what he saw made him stop in amazement. Dr. Simpson had finished reading his Bible and had begun to pray. But he did not drop to his knees beside the desk, nor did he even bow his head and close his eyes. Instead, he reached out to the end of his desk and pulled toward him a small globe. He began slowly revolving it and praying aloud for all the lost multitudes of earth as the various countries of the world passed before him.

"I felt that I stood on holy ground," testified the visitor, and then his awe and wonder increased at what he saw next.

Dr. Simpson had finished his prayer, his scholarly voice betraying the deep and growing emotion which he felt. Suddenly the distinguished old man put his arms around the globe and hugged it to him, as if trying to love the lost home to God. Then he bent his head over the globe and wept until it seemed to the awed visitor, still watching from the doorway, that the tears that ran freely down Simpson's cheeks struck the top of the globe and there divided so that some went down one side and some down another—until the whole earth was wet with his tears of compassion. Truly here was an enlarged heart![1]

WHO CAN MEASURE THE INFLUENCE of one compassionate heart? Or who can measure the fruitfulness of a life wholly available to God? Only God in eternity! But we are allowed to see just a bit now. From the womb of Dr. Simpson have come mission stations around the world staffed by hundreds of missionaries, as well as hundreds of churches at home and abroad; also several colleges now preparing lives to fulfill their own destiny before God. In this one glimpse, we see ...

A   THE DISTINCTIVE MARK of a man whose heart had gotten so close to the heart of God that it could beat in symphony with His for a lost world. Lord, awaken my heart to share Your burden.

WHO CAN WEIGH ON THE SCALE OF ETERNAL VALUE the worth of any man's work for God! Since God alone knows what He has purposed for him, then He alone can measure whether that man's partnership fulfills what He intended.

Look for a moment at another compassionate heart. All the world remembers how David Livingstone penetrated the dark continent of Africa. Henry Stanley led an expedition to find Livingstone when he had disappeared in the wilds of Africa. Upon finding him, he urged him to return to England where people had begun to recognize the great work of his exploration, and his total dedication to break up the slave trade. Livingstone could have gone back to England to receive great acclaim and to be recognized as one of the great men of the British Empire. But he refused saying, "My work is not yet finished." Reluctantly, Henry Stanley returned alone.

Two days later David Livingstone wrote in his diary: "March 19, my birthday, my Jesus, my King, my life, my all. I again dedicate my whole self to Thee. Accept me and grant, O gracious Father, that ere the year is gone I may finish my work. In Jesus' name I ask it. Amen."

The words of a true servant! Just one year later, David Livingstone's servant found him on his knees beside his cot, dead. His sufferings had increased continually, and upon reaching Chitambo's village in Northern Rhodesia—now Zambia, he died on his knees, May 31st, 1873. The people embalmed his body and carried it amidst the greatest perils to the shore, where it was sent on a cruiser and finally buried in Westminister Abbey.

What sustained Livingstone? It is said that when he had visited Scotland after an absence of sixteen years, he spoke at the University of Glasgow. Now it had always been the custom of undergraduates to have some boyish fun at the expense of visiting dignitaries; and that day they came with pop-guns and pea-shooters. When the students saw Livingstone's gaunt form and dark face, tanned by the African sun and furrowed by the hardship, toil and fever—saw the limp arm hanging by his side—made useless by a lion's bite, they forgot their fun and joined only in the applause. After Livingstone had referred to the honorable careers of most of his classmates, he turned to the young men and he urged them to live a dedicated life.

"Shall I tell you what sustained me in my exiled life, among strangers whose language I could not understand?" he suddenly asked. And then in the hush that followed he said, "It was this that comforted me at all times: 'Lo, I am with you always, even unto the end of the world.'" Every heart that day felt the power of that grand promise. Livingstone was both its witness and its example.

In looking out upon that dark continent with all its slavery, Livingstone was so gripped with the need, that the urgency of his prayers could not be denied. Alone he pioneered a way that millions might receive the light of the gospel. We behold . . .

B ANOTHER DISTINCTIVE MARK: Because Livingstone had long before determined that the plaudits of this world, even though justly earned, were small compared with the joy of his Lord's approval, he with unswerving dedication ignored any personal gain or comfort that he might live unto fullness.

WHEN GOD IS CALLING US TO FULLNESS, be assured he can take one small seed and when planted, cause it to bring forth a hundred-fold. Consider these precious words of a father, who announced one day: "I have nothing too precious for my Lord Jesus. He has asked for my best, and with all my heart, I give my very best to Him."

These words were spoken by a father who was giving his only daughter as a missionary to China. It was at the farewell meeting in Philadelphia, for a number of new missionaries sailing for China. This father did not know at that time that he would never see his daughter again; that she was soon to be with Christ. When that news reached him, through the grace that God gave him, he wrote:

"I can still say I have nothing too precious for my Lord Jesus."

Those words strangely gripped Hudson Taylor when he heard them. Later he said, "They were the richest thing I got in America, and have been an untold blessing to me ever since. Sometimes, when pressed with correspondence, the hour has come for united prayer, and the thought has arisen, ought I not to go on with this or that matter? Then it has come to me—'nothing too precious for my Lord Jesus,' and the correspondence has been left to be cared for later. I could never tell how many hundred times God has given me a blessing through these words."

> THE DISTINCTIVE MARK: Willingness to give one's best to the Lord for Him to use as He will. This unknown father who gave his daughter continues to speak to countless others like Hudson Taylor. Only God can measure the value, and eternity will reveal the impact of one life wholly alive to pleasing God. Oh, awaken my heart to announce with joy, "nothing is too precious for my Lord."

THOSE WHO LIVE UNTO FULLNESS will be pouring themselves into others. I read of a woman who has remained anonymous, who went to an orphanage in Iowa and asked, "Is there an orphan here that nobody wants?" The matron replied, "Indeed, there is. She's ten years old, ugly to look at and has a terrible hunchback. She is sickly, ill-tempered, cross and irritable. The only beautiful thing about her is her name, MERCY GOODFAITH! We have long since given up hope of getting her adopted." That unknown woman replied, "That is exactly the child I want," and took Mercy Goodfaith home with her.

Thirty-five years passed. The head of the Orphanage Inspection Department was checking out orphanages one day. He turned in a report about one particular orphanage, which said, "This orphanage is outstanding, is exquisitely clean. The food is wonderful. And all this is attributed to the matron of the place, out of whose soul there oozes love.

"When I dropped in for an unexpected inspection," he continued, "it was dinner time. At the close of dinner, the matron said, 'Girls and boys, let's do what we always do after dinner,' and with that they all moved into the living room. One of the girls sat at the piano and all the children started singing Christmas songs. The matron herself sat in a big over-stuffed chair with huge arm-rests that were about a foot wide. Two little girls sat on one arm of the chair and two boys on the other, and two other children sat on her lap. From time to time they would stroke the matron's hair. One little child was curled at her feet and played with the silky dress against her lip. Never did I see such beautiful eyes as those in that matron. So beautiful that I almost forgot how ugly her face was and how huge and gruesome was her hunchback. Her name was MERCY GOODFAITH."

Because Mercy Goodfaith had been the object of a self-giving love, she was now multiplying that love manifold. Someday the nameless woman who took her will be revealed to the world. For now, we can only say, this mother was living unto fullness—content to be known only to God.

D   ANOTHER DISTINCTIVE MARK stands out—a willingness to pour your life and love into another.

THERE ARE OTHERS we should mention! Dr. Henry Poppen, who spent over forty years as a missionary to China, once shared his experience of going to a remote village, where presumably missionaries had never been. There he told the people about Jesus, that He was gentle and kind, that He was able to forgive easily, and that He loved even those who were unloveable.

When Dr. Poppen finished telling the villagers about Jesus, some of the men came to him and said, "We know Jesus! He has been here!"

"No," said Dr. Poppen. "He lived and died in a country that is far away from here."

"No! no!" they insisted, "He died here. Come, we'll show you his grave."

They led him outside the city to a cemetary where only one American was buried. There on the tombstone was the name of a Christian medical doctor, who, all on his own, felt called by Jesus Christ to go there, live there, and die there. Now the people were sure he was Jesus; the very person Dr. Poppen described had to be He.

Unknown! Unheralded for great exploits—but known by God, and by those who had "touched him." Some day we shall know who he was. Thus we behold . . .

E   ANOTHER DISTINCTIVE MARK: A contentment to wait for God's day of rewarding. It does indeed require a real working of the Cross to find your satisfaction in the Lord.

MUCH HAS BEEN WRITTEN about the unusual prayer-ministry of Praying Hyde, the man whose intercession shook India. In fact wherever he went, God moved mightily. Evangelist J. Wilbur

Chapman explains how God graciously used Praying Hyde to help them.

"In one of our missions in England when the audience was extremely small, results seemed impossible. Then I received a note saying that an American missionary was coming to town who would pray God's blessing upon our work. He was known as Praying Hyde.

"Almost instantly the tide turned. The hall was packed, and my first invitation meant fifty men for Jesus Christ. As we were leaving I said, 'Mr. Hyde, I want you to pray for me.' He came to my room, turned the key in the door, dropped to his knees, waited five minutes without a single syllable coming from his lips. I could hear my own heart thumping and beating; I felt the hot tears running down my face. I knew I was with God. Then with upturned face, down which the tears were streaming, he said, 'Oh, God!'

"For five minutes at least, he was still again, and then when he knew he was talking with God his arm went round my shoulder and there came up from the depth of his heart such petitions for men as I had never heard before. I rose from my knees to know what real prayer was."

No one need wonder why this man became known around the world as mighty Praying Hyde. All who got near him knew his burden for souls, and God's willingness to answer him. People also came to realize his was no ordinary kind of praying—it could better be called "desperation-pleading". Yes, this is

F
ANOTHER DISTINCTIVE MARK of living unto fullness: We become so one-with-God's heart burden that we can know what is His will and boldly take our answer.

SUCH DESPERATION KNOWS NO CLOSED DOORS! "It is time we sought God's definition of a closed door and forget some of our own," writes R. Arthur Matthews. "When we hear the wolves howling, we think we have to rush for cover, lest we get hurt. Jesus saw things the other way. He said to His disciples, 'I send you as sheep into the midst of wolves.' We are not justified in arguing that a door is closed just because danger is threatening. Paul's reasoning endorses the Savior's remarks. He says, 'Buy up the opportunity, because the days are evil.' "It was this that gave Watchman Nee his text when he returned to Shanghai under the communists in 1949 and found many of his friends preparing to escape. He himself was outside China at the time of Mao's takeover and could have stayed in the free world if he had heeded the advice of his friends. But in prayer God had showed him that his responsibility lay in China. Daniel was taken captive to his assignment—he had no choice as to place. Watchman Nee was captive in another sense, as he declared his intention of going back into the lion's den."(2)

During his long years of imprisonment, many of us waited and prayed eagerly for the time Watchman Nee might be released to minister outside China. Millions throughout the world waited to see and hear personally the man whose writings had such depth and yet simplicity. But it was apparently not in God's plan. After more than twenty years of imprisonment by the communists in Shanghai, the Lord took him home. What a testimony his life and writings have been to millions. In this veteran of the Cross we see yet . . .

G   ANOTHER DISTINCTIVE MARK: Embracing the way of the Cross means accepting the danger, the unknown, and a willingness like Paul to pay any price to fulfill our calling to gain the prize.

WHO CAN MEASURE ANY LIFE that is deliberately pressing to fulfill all God's will in his generation? Recently in a survey made by LEADERSHIP magazine among pastors and workers, Nee's book, RELEASE OF THE SPIRIT, was listed among the top ten as a book that had most affected their personal life and ministry. We share this to remind you that even though a man is isolated away in prison, God will have His way. While most of the writings of Nee have come from his spoken ministry before his imprisonment, God continues to use him in blessing multitudes who read his books.

In the last letter Watchman Nee wrote to his niece (which was forwarded on to friends in New York) he encouraged her by saying: "Do not be concerned for me; I have learned how to maintain my joy." What a testimony from a man who had survived long years of poor health, suffering and imprisonment by the enemy. Yes, Lord, AWAKEN OUR HEARTS to realize that true joy is not governed by circumstances, but in knowing You as our Source. Thus shall we be enabled to finish our race . . . not somehow . . . but triumphantly.

WE HAVE LISTED THE DISTINCTIVE MARKS of some who were well-known and others wholly unknown, except to God. How much we want to assume that each of these lived UNTO

FULLNESS. Only God knows! Yet we can rejoice in this: Our Father looks with much joy upon every one of His children who has set his heart to please Him and finish his race triumphantly.

HOW SHALL WE EXPLAIN these stalwart men and women whom we admire? Is there some secret common to all—something we can get hold of to help explain their living unto fullness?. Yes, there is this ONE MESSAGE we have sought to emphasize. Miss this, and you have missed the central burden of our journey together:

FELLOWSHIP WITH GOD CAN ONLY BE SUSTAINED AS WE DEVELOP ROOTS IN HIM.

Let us look back over our journey together these 15 days and summarize the lessons we are learning. Perhaps I can help establish five principles in your memory by using these five letters: R–O–O–T–S as emphasized by five key words. If you will, for a moment, just think of binding a letter to each one of your fingers and your thumb. Consider first, the letter R.

RESPONDING: Learning to respond to God properly in every life-situation is the first step. Remember when the storms of life come, yours can be a REACTION that ruins your own life and affects all those around you. Or you can learn to RESPOND to God and let your roots go down to take freely from the river of His grace. Perhaps some of our lesson titles will help you recall what we have meant by properly responding:

Recognizing the importance of our Helper;

Joyfully accepting all God's ways;

Becoming more attentive in our hearing.

OBEDIENCE: You will remember Corrie Ten Boom told us her simple way for receiving God's supply of strength when she faced something most difficult. She explained it was her willingness to obey. Corrie called this the ONE PRIOR CONDITION. We can see this same determination to obey God at any cost, as a distinctive mark of all who live unto fullness.

OCCUPATION: I am convinced that most of God's children too easily get their attention diverted, and they become occupied with secondary things. For example, as we have read in today's lesson of Simpson, Livingstone, Taylor, Praying Hyde or Watchman Nee—

we could allow these distinctive marks we see in them to overwhelm us. To measure ourselves by their achievements would only bring despair. Be careful! God has not called us to walk in their calling. Therefore, we must be careful to only glance at them and keep our heart-gaze upon the Lord Jesus. Yes, look at all these who left an imprint on their generation, but keep our eyes "fixed upon the Lord Jesus." As we RESPOND to Him, walk in simple OBEDIENCE to Him, and keep OCCUPIED with Him, God will accomplish the necesary . . .

TRAINING we all need. Remember the years Joe Evans spent in God's schoolroom; remember the patience of John Wright Follette as he joyfully accepted God's ways in dealing with his family; all of us can rejoice that even in the most severe trials and testings, God will help us develop a root-life that experiences His abundant supply from the river of His grace. Yes, we can either be offended with God's dealings and react, or we can accept His TRAINING as a responder. Finally, as our roots go down in deeper fellowship, we can . . .

STAND with Him. You remember how the team with Watchman Nee faced the entrenched Enemy who had controlled the island as a stronghold for years. To know God as our Father, as our Provider, as our Sovereign, as our VICTOR is wonderful. To be utterly yielded to Him for fulfilling all His purposes is necessary, but to know how to STAND WITH HIM IN ALL HIS WAYS has become our central concern in this journey. Why not bind these five words to your fingers. Ask God to develop your root-life: RESPONDING, OBEDIENCE, OCCUPATION, TRAINING AND STANDING. As these become operative in you, your race will be triumph unto Him.

LIVING UNTO FULLNESS . . . OF PURPOSE

In our diagram we have pictured the PURPOSE BOX at the end of life's journey. Since our fellowship with God is not an end in itself, but a means to His End, then what is that glorious End or purpose? The best answer will come from the words of the apostle Paul:

> For God has allowed us to know the secret of His Plan, and it is this: He purposes in His sovereign will that all human history shall be consummated in Christ, that everything that exists in

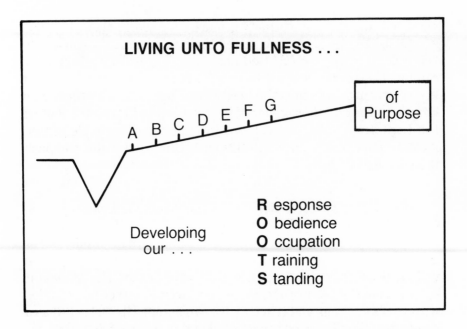

LIVING UNTO FULLNESS . . .

A B C D E F G

of Purpose

Developing our . . .

R esponse
O bedience
O ccupation
T raining
S tanding

Heaven or earth shall find its perfection and fulfillment in Him. And here is the staggering thing—that in all which will one day belong to Him we have been promised a share (since we were long ago destined for this by the One who achieves His purposes by His sovereign Will), so that we, as the first to put our confidence in Christ, may bring praise to His glory! (Eph.1:10-12 Phillips).

PAUL EXPLAINS TO THE SAINTS IN ROME that our present distress is temporary and negligible:

In my opinion whatever we may have to go through now is less than nothing compared with the magnificent future God has planned for us . . . (Rom.8:18 Phillips).

And it is plain, too, that we who have a foretaste of the Spirit are in a state of painful tension, while we wait for that redemption of our bodies which will mean that at last we have realized our full sonship in Him (Rom.8:23 Phillips).

Moreover we know that to those who love God, who are called according to His Plan, everything that happens fits into a pattern for good. God, in his foreknowledge, chose them to BEAR THE FAMILY LIKENESS OF HIS SON . . . (Rom.8:28 Phillips). (capitals mine)

IN VIEW OF BEING CALLED INTO SUCH A PARTNERSHIP, we can understand why Paul is pressing toward God's goal:

> Yes, and I look upon everything as loss compared with the overwhelming gain of knowing Christ Jesus my Lord. For his sake I did in actual fact suffer the loss of everything, but I considered it useless rubbish compared with being able to win Christ. For now my place is in Him, and I am not dependent upon any of the self-achieved righteousness of the Law. God has given me that genuine righteousness which comes from faith in Christ.
>
> How changed are my ambitions!
>
> Now I long to know Christ and the power shown by His Resurrection: now I long to share His sufferings, even to die as He died, so that I may perhaps attain, as He did, the resurrection from the dead. Yet my brothers, I do not consider myself to have "arrived" spiritually, nor do I consider myself already perfect. But I keep going on, grasping ever more firmly that purpose for which Christ grasped me.
>
> My brothers, I do not consider myself to have fully grasped it even now. But I do concentrate on this: I leave the past behind and with hands outstretched to whatever lies ahead I go straight for the goal—my reward the honour of being called by God in Christ (Phil.3:8-14 Phillips).

AWAKEN MY HEART to share this same attitude.

Father, I know You have apprehended me for Yourself. Now I want to apprehend that for which I have been apprehended. Like king David, I want to fulfill my unique part in Your purpose for my generation. Let me always be concerned for what You can get from my life before I am concerned for what I can get from You; for when You are fully satisifed, then I shall be satisfied. And I shall know that inner witness, even as Enoch knew, that he pleased God.

I want to thank You, Father, for all those who have joined me on this journey. As we reach this final day, I ask that You will help us to continue this discipline. May we all be filled with new hope and expectation, having set our faces to finish our race triumphantly, and in a greater measure to have realized LIFE'S ULTIMATE PRIVILEGE. Then with . . .

<u>OVERFLOWING GRATITUDE</u> we can sing together . . .

> My goal is God Himself, not joy, nor peace,
>   Nor even blessing, but Himself, my God;
> Tis His to lead me there—not mine, but His—
>   At any cost, dear Lord, by any road.
>
> So faith bounds forward to its goal in God,
>   And love can trust her Lord to lead her there;
> Upheld by Him, my soul is following hard
>   Till God hath full fulfilled my deepest prayer.
>
> No matter if the way be sometimes dark,
>   No matter though the cost be oft-times great,
> He knoweth how I best shall reach the mark,
>   The way that leads to Him must needs be strait.
>
> One thing I know, I cannot say Him nay;
>   One thing I do, I press towards my Lord;
> My God my glory here, from day to day,
>   And in the glory there my great reward.
>   (F. Brook)

PRAYER REQUESTS   DATE ANSWERED

_____
_____
_____
_____
_____
_____
_____
_____
_____
_____
_____
_____
_____
_____
_____
_____
_____
_____
_____
_____

INSIGHTS FROM LESSON

_____
_____
_____
_____
_____
_____
_____
_____
_____
_____
_____
_____
_____
_____
_____
_____
_____
_____

Acknowledgements

DAY 1 ... (1) SELECTED-(author unknown) THE SUNSHINE MAGAZINE

DAY 2 ... (1) H.A.Ironside, ILLUSTRATIONS OF BIBLE TRUTH, © 1945 Moody Bible Institute of Chicago
(2) POWER FOR LIVING magazine, Feb.21,1965.

DAY 3 ... (1) Wentworth Pike in THE PRAIRIE OVERCOMER, Prairie Bible Institute; Three Hills, Alta, Canada TOM 2A0.
(2) G.H.C.Macgregor, TRUE PRAYING IN THE HOLY SPIRIT, The Great Commission Prayer League-1978.
(3) Catherine Marshall, THE HELPER © 1978 Catherine Marshall, Chosen Books Pub.Co.Ltd.
(4) A.W.Tozer, TOZER PULPIT (c) 1968, Christian Publications, Inc. Harrisburg, Pa.17101

DAY 4 ... (1) Dr. Helen Roseveare in THE PRAIRIE OVERCOMER, Prairie Bible Institute, Three Hills, Alta, Canada TOM 2A0
(2) Catherine Marshall in INTERCESSORS, prayer circular © Breakthrough Inc. Lincoln, Va. 22078

DAY 5 ... (1) H.A.Ironside, ILLUSTRATIONS OF BIBLE TRUTH
(2) Wentworth Pike in THE PRAIRIE OVERCOMER,
(3) Peter Lord, THE 2959 PLAN © 1976 AGAPE MINISTRIES 2600 Park Avenue, Titusville, Fl. 32780
(4) John R. Rice, PRAYER, ASKING AND RECEIVING © 1942, Sword of the Lord Publishers

DAY 6 ... (1) Peter Deyneka Jr. CHRISTIANS IN THE SHADOW OF THE KREMLIN © 1974, David C. Cook, Pub. Co.
(2) Diane Scimone in NEW WINE MAGAZINE, Oct. 1985
(3) Same as above

DAY 7 ... (1) V.Raymond Edman, OUT OF MY LIFE, page 103 © 1961 Zondervan Pub. Co. Grand Rapids, Mi.
(2) Watchman Nee, TABLE IN THE WILDERNESS (Jan.30th) Christian Lit. Crusade, Ft. Wash. Pa.19034

DAY 8 . . . (1) D.A.Dowd, Adapted from a tract.

(2) V.Raymond Edman, OUT OF MY LIFE, page 185 © 1961 Zondervan Pub. Co. Grand Rapids, Mi.

DAY 9 . . . (1) Corrie Ten Boom, MARCHING ORDERS FOR THE END BATTLE, ©1969, Christian Lit. Crusade, Ft. Wash. Pa.

(2) Same as above

(3) Same as above

(4) Same as above

DAY 10 . . (1) Peter Lord, THE 2959 PLAN-PRAYER MANUAL.

(2) Corrie Ten Boom, (same as above).

DAY 11 . . (1) John Wright Follette, ARROWS OF TRUTH © Gospel Pub. House, Springfield, Mo.

DAY 12 . . (1) Elda Mills, Bread Upon the Waters, in GUIDEPOSTS. Reprinted by permission from Guideposts Magazine. ©1981, Guideposts Assoc.Inc. Carmel, N.Y. 10512

(2) Ernie Gruen, FREEDOM TO GROW ©1983 Whitaker House Publishers, Springdale, Pa.

DAY 13 . . (1) Watchman Nee, SIT, WALK, STAND © Angus Kinnear, Christian Lit. Crusade, Ft. Wash. Pa.

DAY 14 . . (1) Compiled by S.B.Shaw in 1894. Out of print book, TOUCHING INCIDENTS AND REMARKABLE ANSWERS TO PRAYER.

(3) Judson Cornwall, LET US WORSHIP ©1983 Bridge Pub. Co. So. Plainfield, N.J.

DAY 15 . . (1) Wm.B.Young, Tract WORLD FOCUS. Used by courtesy of New Tribes Mission.

(2) R.Arthur Matthews, BORN FOR BATTLE, © 1978, Overseas Missionary Fellowship.